PAYING THE MODERN MILITARY

Studies in Defense Policy
TITLES IN PRINT

MARTIN BINKIN *and* IRENE KYRIAKOPOULOS

PAYING THE MODERN MILITARY

THE BROOKINGS INSTITUTION
Washington, D.C.

Library of Congress Cataloging in Publication data:
Binkin, Martin, 1928–
  Paying the modern military.
  (Studies in defense policy)
  1. United States—Armed Forces—Pay, allowances,
etc. 2. United States—Armed Forces—Recruiting,
enlistment, etc. 3. Pensions, Military—United
States. I. Kyriakopoulos, Irene, joint author.
II. Title. III. Series.
UC74.B58   355.6′4′0973   80-70080
ISBN 0-8157-0971-4 (pbk.)

9 8 7 6 5 4 3 2 1

THE BROOKINGS INSTITUTION is an independent organization devoted to nonpartisan research, education, and publication in economics, government, foreign policy, and the social sciences generally. Its principal purposes are to aid in the development of sound public policies and to promote public understanding of issues of national importance.

The Institution was founded on December 8, 1927, to merge the activities of the Institute for Government Research, founded in 1916, the Institute of Economics, founded in 1922, and the Robert Brookings Graduate School of Economics and Government, founded in 1924.

The Board of Trustees is responsible for the general administration of the Institution, while the immediate direction of the policies, program, and staff is vested in the President, assisted by an advisory committee of the officers and staff. The by-laws of the Institution state: "It is the function of the Trustees to make possible the conduct of scientific research, and publication, under the most favorable conditions, and to safeguard the independence of the research staff in the pursuit of their studies and in the publication of the results of such studies. It is not a part of their function to determine, control, or influence the conduct of particular investigations or the conclusions reached."

The President bears final responsibility for the decision to publish a manuscript as a Brookings book. In reaching his judgment on the competence, accuracy, and objectivity of each study, the President is advised by the director of the appropriate research program and weighs the views of a panel of expert outside readers who report to him in confidence on the quality of the work. Publication of a work signifies that it is deemed a competent treatment worthy of public consideration but does not imply endorsement of conclusions or recommendations.

The Institution maintains its position of neutrality on issues of public policy in order to safeguard the intellectual freedom of the staff. Hence interpretations or conclusions in Brookings publications should be understood to be solely those of the authors and should not be attributed to the Institution, to its trustees, officers, or other staff members, or to the organizations that support its research.

FOREWORD

As THE United States enters the 1980s, there is a gathering consensus that the nation's military capabilities are faltering, in no small part a result of problems in manning the armed services. Difficulties in attracting qualified volunteers and mounting losses of experienced specialists and technicians have prompted calls for a return to conscription, for reductions in the size of the armed forces, or for increases in military pay and benefits.

In this study, the twenty-second in the Brookings series on defense policy, Martin Binkin and Irene Kyriakopoulos argue that without paying the social, military, or financial costs that such alternatives would impose, the nation can take steps to increase substantially the return on its present investment in the military payroll.

In their preceding study, *Youth or Experience? Manning the Modern Military,* the authors contended that the U.S. military establishment's emphasis on youth and vigor has yielded armed forces too inexperienced to operate and maintain today's sophisticated weapon systems and has institutionalized policies and practices that make change exceedingly difficult. Chief among the obstacles to improvement is a pay arrangement that remunerates members of the armed forces on the basis of rank and longevity and according to their "needs." Because it does little to recognize differences in the value of occupational qualifications—distinctions that civilian pay systems have always emphasized—military pay is especially attractive to personnel with less valuable skills, while it fails to satisfy those with the more valuable skills. The armed forces, as a result, tend to lose the people they need to keep and to keep the people they can afford to lose.

In this study the authors propose that the tight bond between rank and pay be loosened. They contend that pay rates tied more closely to occupation, job setting, investment in training, and alternative job opportunities in the civilian economy would result in higher retention rates and longer tenure among skilled personnel.

Adoption of a more efficient pay policy, according to the authors, should be accompanied by reform of the military retirement system, which indiscriminately encourages service members to seek career status, to serve twenty years, and to retire shortly thereafter. They argue that an occupation-based pay structure would promote the selective retention of skilled personnel, leaving the way clear to design a more equitable and efficient retirement system.

Martin Binkin and Irene Kyriakopoulos are members of the research staff of the Brookings Foreign Policy Studies program. They are grateful to Donald G. Ogilvie and R. James Woolsey for helpful comments during the preparation of the manuscript, as well as to Robert F. Hale, Leon Hirsh, William M. Hix, Fred McCoy, John W. Nicholson, and Alan W. Swinger.

The authors also thank their Brookings colleagues Robert W. Hartman and John D. Steinbruner for valuable suggestions, Alice M. Carroll for editing the manuscript, Clifford A. Wright for verifying its factual content, and Ann M. Ziegler for bearing the secretarial burden.

The Institution acknowledges the assistance of the Ford Foundation and the Rockefeller Foundation, whose grants helped to support this study. The views expressed here are those of the authors and should not be ascribed to the persons who commented on the manuscript, to the Ford Foundation or the Rockefeller Foundation, or to the trustees, officers, or other staff members of the Brookings Institution.

BRUCE K. MAC LAURY
President

November 1980
Washington, D.C.

CONTENTS

Text Tables

Appendix Tables

CHAPTER ONE

THE CENTRAL ISSUES

THE VAGUE RESTLESSNESS that developed in the late 1970s over the United States' military vulnerabilities has given way to deep concern in the 1980s. According to a large and growing body of critics, U.S. armed forces are beset by a variety of problems, not the least of which is the recruitment and retention of men and women qualified to run a technologically complex military establishment. A ground swell of support has emerged for some form of action to correct the deficiencies; some propose increases in military pay and benefits, others advocate a return to conscription, and still others argue for reductions in the size of the nation's armed forces. One or more of these measures may ultimately prove necessary, but before paying the financial, social, or national security costs associated with these options, it is important to ensure that the nation extracts the maximum return from its investment in the military payroll.

Recruitment

Whether or not the United States could raise its armed forces by voluntary means has been a controversial issue ever since military conscription was abolished in 1973. Critics have feared that not enough men and women willing and able to volunteer would be found unless the nation was prepared to incur exorbitant budgetary costs or to compromise the quality and therefore the effectiveness of its armed forces.

For the first several years without conscription, the armed services, with few exceptions, were able to attract the number of new recruits they sought. Some heralded these achievements as an indication that voluntary recruitment was indeed a feasible proposition, while skeptics attributed this success to a modest but steady decline in the size of the armed forces, a relatively large youth population, and a worsening economy. But there was little agitation for change.

Toward the end of the 1970s, as détente became strained and there were signs that the Soviet Union was engaged in a major military buildup, concern about military recruitment grew. Critics pointed to worsening recruitment shortfalls in the active forces and even greater manning problems in the reserve components; to growing racial overrepresentation in the Army and Marine Corps; to the declining "quality" of recruits (as measured by level of education and by standardized test scores). And, more and more, the imminent decline in the youth population as the baby boom ran its course was expected to hamper military recruitment.

By 1980 a new consensus that the volunteer force was in trouble began to emerge. Even so ardent a supporter of voluntarism as Melvin R. Laird, former secretary of defense and one of the architects of the volunteer experiment, acknowledged the deteriorating manpower situation:

Recruiting and retention targets have been revised downward each year [since 1973]. . . . When we ended the draft, the size of our force stood at 2.3 million but we had confidence that this level or higher could be maintained. Today, it stands at about 2 million, 16 percent below the level of seven years ago. Each year, at least one of the services has missed these declining targets, and last year, for the first time, all four of our armed services failed to meet their recruiting goals.[1]

Mr. Laird pointed out that there were

qualitative shortfalls as well. Last year, the percentage of high school graduates joining the military declined by 10 percent. Only a little more than 50 percent of those enlisting in the Army were high school graduates, while the Navy, with its increasingly demanding technology, was forced to accept one person below high school graduation level for every three high school graduates who entered. . . . The quality problem is so bad that, even with a 16,000 person shortfall, 60 percent of the men recruited in fiscal year 1979 by the Army were below the national average in intelligence.[2]

The Carter administration, breaking with its generally sanguine stance on the all-volunteer force, also noted that in fiscal 1979 "each Service failed to meet its accession goal. . . . There is some concern . . . that the

1. Melvin R. Laird, *People, Not Hardware: The Highest Defense Priority,* AEI Special Analysis 80-1 (Washington, D.C.: American Enterprise Institute, 1980), p. 4.

2. Ibid. To the extent that a high proportion of recruits scoring below the average on standardized tests is viewed as a problem, the situation is even worse than Mr. Laird indicated. In July 1980 the Defense Department divulged that as a result of calibration errors, many of the test scores reported since 1976 had been overstated. U.S. Department of Defense, *Aptitude Testing of Recruits,* Report to the House Committee on Armed Services (Office of the Assistant Secretary of Defense, 1980).

FY 1979 recruiting results may reflect the beginning of a declining trend."[3]

Despite the convergence of views that the all-volunteer force is headed for trouble (if indeed it is not already in it), there is little agreement as to the remedy. Senator John C. Stennis, chairman of the Senate Armed Services Committee and one of the principal proponents of the reinstitution of conscription, argues that

Congress has joined the military leaders in trying to make the all-volunteer concept work. There have been large increases in pay. . . . But still we cannot get enough of the right kind of people. . . . It is time for us to reconsider and, after careful appraisal and study, to move to a new type of selective service that will be fair and equitable to all.[4]

Others have proposed broader "national service" options. Representative Paul N. McCloskey, Jr., introduced legislation in 1979 to establish a national service system under which individuals could choose to do voluntary military or civilian service or be inducted into military service by random selection.[5] Senator Sam Nunn, chairman of the Senate Armed Services Manpower and Personnel Subcommittee, has emerged as the Senate's most ardent proponent of national service. He has suggested that "a minimally coercive national service organization might require each young person to register at 18 years of age and attend an orientation program designed to encourage participation in some form of national service, such as the Job Corps, VISTA, environmental reclamation, or the armed forces."[6]

Those who remain philosophically committed to the all-volunteer force argue that recruitment difficulties can be overcome if incentives are strengthened. The centerpiece of a solution proposed by Melvin Laird, for example, is "a national commitment to maintain an acceptable standard of living and a meaningful quality of home life for those who are willing to dedicate their lives to the defense of this country."[7] One of his recommendations would involve an across-the-board pay increase to restore military pay to its 1972 real income levels and another would tie military pay in the future to changes in the consumer price index to protect the

---

3. *Department of Defense Annual Report Fiscal Year 1981*, pp. 264–66.

4. John C. Stennis, "We Need to Draft Enough Good Men," *Newsday* (Long Island), April 5, 1979.

5. *Congressional Record*, daily edition, February 15, 1979, pp. E541–42.

6. Sam Nunn, "Another Look at the All-Volunteer Force," *Washington Post*, March 28, 1977.

7. Laird, *People, Not Hardware*, p. 16.

purchasing power of members of the armed forces. Acknowledging that such initiatives would be expensive ("billions of dollars a year"), Mr. Laird argues that the additional expenditures "must be borne no matter what the cost."[8]

Retention

Usually lost in the debate over recruitment, however, has been the close, albeit subtle, link between the requirement for new people and the retention of those already in the armed forces. Indeed, the number of new recruits the services need depends largely on how willing and able they are to retain their trained members. There are strong signs that military leaders have come to recognize the importance of that relationship, mainly because the armed forces are now faced with what is deemed to be their most significant manpower problem: their inability to retain skilled workers. One of the nation's top military leaders, Admiral Thomas B. Hayward, believes that "if we are concerned about the readiness of our forces worldwide today—and we surely are—nothing is more essential than to stem the exodus of our trained professionals."[9] And in writing to Secretary of Defense Harold Brown in 1979 about the Navy's recruitment shortfalls, he stressed that "a far more serious problem, in the enlisted area is our decline in retention . . . [which] is having a pronounced effect on our ability to maintain necessary enlisted strength in the supervisory grades, E5–E9. . . . We are currently approximately 20,000 petty officers short of the number required to provide the experience level needed."[10]

Retention is also one of the principal difficulties the Air Force faces. According to General Lew Allen, Jr., Chief of Staff, the Air Force faces "serious problems in attracting and, more important, in keeping adequate numbers of qualified and experienced people in the 1980s."[11] In fact, all of the services are troubled by the loss of trained workers. According to one account: "For the last several weeks, the nation's senior military and

8. Ibid., p. 18.

9. U.S. Department of the Navy, Office of Information, "A Matter of Priority," *Navy Policy Briefs,* February 1980, p. 3.

10. Memorandum, Admiral Thomas B. Hayward to Secretary of Defense Harold Brown, "Retention Impact of Personnel Shortfalls," December 13, 1979.

11. Department of the Air Force, "Presentation to the Committee on Armed Services, United States Senate: Statement of General Lew Allen, Jr.," February 1980, p. 7.

naval officers have been marching up to Capitol Hill to sound an alarm: The armed services are rapidly losing their best and most experienced personnel." The exodus, it is maintained, "has done more to weaken the military readiness of the United States than shortages of guns or gasoline."[12]

The concern is well justified. Retention rates are crucial determinants of force size and force quality as well. The relationship—indeed, the interaction—between retention and recruitment rates is inherent in the nature of the military personnel system which allows for entry only at the bottom of the institution's hierarchy. In such a closed system more than one individual must be recruited for every trained worker who is *not* retained. This happens because of attrition; there are always some trainees who "wash out," and their replacement involves the training of a proportionally greater number of recruits. It has been estimated that, on the basis of very conservative assumptions, for every 100 enlisted job vacancies the military needs to recruit, process, and train at least 120 new entrants.[13] The recruitment-retention ratio in the Navy, however, has been put as high as 5 to 1 (that is, five new recruits would be needed to offset the loss of one trained jobholder).[14]

It follows that personnel losses have a doubly adverse impact on force readiness. "Low-retention begets falling manning levels which generate increased accessions and training requirements which in turn increase personnel requirements. . . . Overworked, undersupervised crews represent poor retention prospects, and this brings us back to the start of the cycle."[15]

Even more significant, however, is the effect on the quality of the military work force. For the military, retaining trained workers is essentially the only way in which they can preserve a pool of skilled journeymen and supervisors. By tradition, the military do not recruit trained journeymen; rather, they concentrate on developing skills by offering extensive training (formal as well as on-the-job) to new entrants. This tradition, in conjunction with the armed forces' growing need for specialists, has become a costly proposition; about $3 billion a year, or about 10

12. *New York Times*, March 22, 1980.

13. Martin Binkin and Irene Kyriakopoulos, *Youth or Experience? Manning the Modern Military* (Brookings Institution, 1979), p. 60.

14. Admiral Thomas B. Hayward is reported to have stated: "If I retained 4,000 more mid-grade petty officers" each year, "that's 20,000 new recruits who would not have to be trained to take their place." *Washington Post*, November 8, 1979.

15. Memorandum, Admiral Hayward to Secretary Brown.

percent of the military personnel appropriation, is expended just to maintain the enlisted training pipeline.[16] To realize the full returns to such an investment, of course, requires that workers be retained long enough in their jobs to acquire expertise and, ultimately, to use it.

Retention rates, then, determine the overall level of experience of the force—the skill and know-how of military personnel, and their ability to perform the myriad of tasks that defense now involves. Indeed, it is the nature of modern military tasks that makes retention rates significant and the implications of their decline so alarming for force readiness. The transformation of the military occupational structure accounts in large measure for the manpower development effort that the armed forces must undertake and for the crucial role that retention plays.

Technology and Military Occupations

Advances in technology since World War II have had a dramatic influence on the U.S. defense establishment.[17] Unlike the armed forces of an earlier period that were dominated by combat operatives—infantrymen and fighting ships' companies—the vast majority of military personnel today are involved in supporting the combat mission.

The shift away from work requiring general military skills toward tasks requiring special skills is reflected in the overall growth in the proportion of personnel trained in white-collar occupations. The latter now account for 46 percent of the total compared to 28 percent in 1945, mirroring the growth in white-collar employment in the economy as a whole. In the military the change has occurred in the technical fields, which now require computer specialists, electronics technicians, medical technologists, and the like. And even clerical workers, whose share of military jobs has remained relatively stable over the years, must be familiar with the use and operation of data processing systems.

Among blue-collar enlisted workers, who in 1978 constituted 55 percent of the military labor force, compared with 72 percent in 1945, similar shifts have occurred, mainly because of the sharp decrease in the percentage of ground combat soldiers. Craftsmen accounted for 27 percent of all enlisted workers in 1978 and about half of all blue-collar military per-

16. Binkin and Kyriakopoulos, *Youth or Experience?* p. 54.
17. For a discussion of the impact of technology on the occupational structure of the armed forces see ibid., chap. 3. The evolution of the mix of jobs in the armed forces is illustrated in appendix table A-1, below.

sonnel. By contrast, only 40 percent of blue-collar workers were craftsmen in 1945. The duties of these military craftsmen include repair and maintenance of equipment, installation and maintenance of utilities, and general construction.

The ascendancy of technicians and specialists over warriors that technological substitution has brought about in the armed forces has so industrialized the military institution that a large segment of it now resembles civilian organizations. The evidence indicates that, contrary to perceived stereotypes, not only does the defense sector have a significant number of occupations in common with the civil sector but the proportion of technical and craft workers is greater in the military.[18] In particular, the percentage of jobs in the armed services that require technical skills is almost twice as large as in the rest of the economy. Over a quarter of all positions for enlisted personnel fall in the category of crafts, while only 13 percent of civilian workers are craftsmen; and even when only the male civilian work force is considered, still only about a fifth of its members are employed as craftsmen.

The Experience Mix

Clearly the armed forces' need for trained, experienced personnel is much greater and more pressing today than in the 1940s and, by necessity, the length of service consistent with the military's training investment in people much longer. But the need is hardly being met.

The lack of experience that characterizes the military work force is reflected in the age profile of enlisted personnel. Of some 1.8 million enlisted individuals on the rolls in 1977 (as compared to about 300,000 officers), 60 percent were under twenty-five years old and close to 90 percent were under thirty-five. This age profile is inconsistent with the high concentration of technical and craft jobs in the military, the training investment required to fill them, and the importance of the defense mission. The need for a higher level of experience than that in the rest of the economy would imply that the military relied on seasoned, mature workers to a greater extent than civilian employers do. Yet, this is not the case, as table 1-1 shows; the more heavily industrialized armed forces rely on a much younger and hence less experienced work force than does the civilian sector.

18. See appendix table A-2.

Table 1-1. Distribution of Military Enlisted Personnel and Civilian Sector Employed Workers, by Age, 1977

Percent

Category	Age				
	Under 20	*20–24*	*25–34*	*35–44*	*Over 44*
Military enlisted personnel	18	42	27	11	1
Civilian sector					
Employed workers	8	14	26	19	33
Male workers	8	13	26	19	34

Sources: Based on data provided by U.S. Department of Defense, Office of Assistant Secretary of Defense for Manpower, Reserve Affairs, and Logistics; *Employment and Training Report of the President, 1978*, table A-14, p. 202. Percentages are rounded.

The disproportionate dependence of the armed forces on youth and consequently their failure to realize the experience potential of their work force are not recent phenomena. Similar patterns of manpower utilization prevailed at least as far back as 1920 and the median age of military personnel has remained relatively unchanged since then.[19]

Imbalances and Their Implications

Viewed in conjunction with the evolution in the occupational structure of the armed forces, that pattern of personnel utilization, which had become inappropriate by the 1960s, now appears completely obsolete and counterproductive. If staffing practices in the civilian sector are any indication, the occupational requirements of the armed forces and the experience profile of its work force are far from matched. Comparison of the age distribution of military personnel to that of employed males in the civilian sector shows that the civilian sector relies on experienced workers to a much greater extent than the armed forces do across the whole occupational spectrum.[20]

Quite apart from the comparison with the civilian sector, the military's lack of mature workers has consequences for the level of military effectiveness. More and more, military managers are acknowledging the difficulty of manning the forces with people lacking the experience needed for efficient performance of the complex technical tasks demanded by modern technology. According to the chief of naval personnel, the "most critical retention problems and shortfalls are [among] those personnel with generally seven to twelve years of service. . . . This shortfall, coupled with

19. See appendix table A-3.
20. See appendix table A-4.

our existing experienced personnel shortages of about 16,000 in the 8–17th year of service at the end of FY 1977, significantly impact on fleet readiness."[21]

These imbalances appear to be getting worse as the surpluses of apprentices and helpers grow larger and the shortfalls of senior technicians and specialists greater when measured in terms of percent of required personnel on hand at the various pay grades:[22]

Pay grade	1962	1967	1972	1977
E-1 through E-3	123	110	122	176
E-4 through E-6	90	86	96	92
E-7 through E-9	93	93	95	89

Poor retention rates would have most serious implications for readiness in those services that, because of occupational orientation, rely most heavily on experienced personnel—the Air Force and the Navy. For the latter, a recent assessment reveals a disturbing trend in the number of ships whose combat readiness is severely restricted by shortages of experienced personnel:[23]

Personnel readiness	November 1977	November 1978	November 1979
Marginally combat ready	56	44	68
Not combat ready	11	9	28
Total	67	53	96

21. Statement of Vice Admiral James D. Watkins, Chief of Naval Personnel and Deputy Chief of Naval Operations for Manpower, *Department of Defense Authorization for Appropriations for Fiscal Year 1979,* Hearings before the Senate Committee on Armed Services, 95 Cong. 2 sess. (Government Printing Office, 1978), pt. 4: *Manpower and Personnel,* pp. 2823–24.

22. Rolf H. Clark, "Resource Allocations in the U.S. Navy: Perspectives and Prospects" (July 1978).

23. Memorandum, Admiral Hayward to Secretary Brown. Combat readiness, which depends on a variety of quantitative and qualitative measurements, falls into five categories: fully combat ready; substantially combat ready; marginally combat ready; not combat ready; and programmed to be not combat ready. A ship considered to be marginally combat ready "has major deficiencies in its prescribed levels of wartime resources or training which limit its capability to perform the wartime mission for which it is organized, designed, or tasked. It can deploy or execute its operational contingency mission at reduced capability, but normally it will first be given additional training or resources to increase its readiness posture." A ship considered to be not combat ready "has major deficiencies in prescribed wartime resources or cannot perform the wartime mission for which it is organized, designed, or tasked. It requires major upgrading prior to deployment or employment in combat. However, if conditions dictate, the unit might be deployed or employed for whatever capability it does possess." Joint Chiefs of Staff, Policy Memorandum 172, January 19, 1979.

For his part, Air Force Secretary Hans Mark is reported to be concerned that "airplanes don't fly because we don't have maintenance people"[24]—experienced maintenance people, needless to say.

Though it is difficult to precisely gauge military effectiveness, research results indicate a very strong link between experience and effectiveness in a military setting. A 1957 study concluded that

as the tools of modern defense and the technology of their use become more intricately complex, men—the human element in defense—become more, not less important. Greater numbers of men do not satisfy this need. Only marked increases in the level of competence and experience of the men in the force can provide for the effective, economical operation required by the changing times and national needs. . . . without the control of the skilled individual the weapon is only an inert, complicated and expensive device.[25]

This statement applies with even greater force in the 1980s. As the *Defense Resource Management Study* observed, in a report requested by President Carter and submitted to the secretary of defense in 1979, "a more experienced force . . . would be better able to absorb and train new personnel required to reconstitute and sustain the combat forces . . . in most NATO/Warsaw Pact scenarios. . . . Increasing the experience level in a pool of flight-line maintenance technicians could dramatically increase a squadron's rapid turnaround capability." The squadron's ability to repair aircraft components would increase the number of mission-ready aircraft and reduce the number that must be kept in inventory.[26]

How is it, then, that the need for experienced military personnel is acknowledged—indeed, stressed by some as even more acute than the need for hardware—yet retention rates are falling? By most accounts the problem can be attributed to the military pay policies of recent years—policies that have not allowed for raises large enough to offset the effects of inflation on the pay of armed forces personnel. This judgment has prompted calls for flat, across-the-board pay increases—to all personnel, in all of the services, in all occupations—which is well in line with established policy.[27] The trouble is, however, that equal percentage adjustments in pay may not be sufficient to correct retention problems; a flat

24. *Wall Street Journal,* March 25, 1980.

25. *Report of the Defense Advisory Committee on Professional and Technical Compensation,* vol. 1: *Military Personnel* (GPO, 1957), pp. 9, 43.

26. Donald B. Rice, *Defense Resource Management Study,* Final Report (GPO, 1979), pp. 66–68.

27. A bill introduced by Senator William Armstrong called for a flat, across-the-board increase in military pay. *Congressional Record,* daily edition, February 4, 1980.

raise in no way guarantees appropriate pay levels to the technicians and specialists the military needs to keep while it unnecessarily increases costs in areas where shortages are nonexistent.

Proponents of *selective* pay increases to military personnel argue that if money is to be spent to improve the manning of the armed forces, the largest raises ought to be granted to those personnel the military can least afford to lose. This marks a departure from established military pay policy. By tradition, retention rates have been controlled—though not necessarily with success—through a system of bonuses administered on an ad hoc basis and separately by each service. But more and more legislators are considering measures aimed at improving retention principally by targeting increases in *pay* toward the career element of the enlisted force —those personnel who have completed at least one term of service.[28] And the recent proposals of the President's Commission on Military Compensation call not only for introducing selective pay increases but also for reforming the military retirement system—thus acknowledging the importance of both pay and retirement benefits as retention devices.[29]

Inasmuch as this indicates a change in future military compensation policy, a broad set of fundamental questions arises. To what extent is the military pay system shaped and implemented on the basis of manning considerations? What impact are changes in pay and retirement benefits likely to have on retention rates? To what degree can the present system of compensation—probably the most powerful manpower policy instrument, yet also the one most deeply anchored in tradition—keep up with the changing needs of the armed forces? Are the structure and composition of compensation—notably pay and retirement benefits—consistent with the manning goals of the modern military establishment?

THIS STUDY after examining the underlying rationale of the current pay system and its principal flaws suggests changes in military pay policy that would relate wages more closely to jobs performed. It goes on to suggest corollary changes in retirement policy that would align the military plan

28. This was the aim of a bill introduced by Senators Sam Nunn and John Warner. Ibid. The 96th Congress, stopping short of imposing selective increases, granted authority to the administration to reallocate by grade and years of service up to 25 percent of the fiscal 1981 pay increase. *Department of Defense Authorization Act, 1981*, S. Rept. 96-895, 96 Cong. 2 sess. (GPO, 1980). The administration, however, chose to apply the October 1, 1980, increase across the board.

29. *Report of the President's Commission on Military Compensation* (GPO, 1978).

more closely with other federal government plans. Taken together—and it is important that they be—these changes would provide the armed forces with the management tools necessary to shape a work force more closely matched to the technological demands of the modern military.

The analysis of the military compensation system is confined to the enlisted component of the armed forces. Enlisted personnel constitute close to 90 percent of total military manpower and account for at least as great a share of the manning problems. But the methodology employed in this study would also be generally applicable to the analysis of compensation in the officer corps.

CHAPTER TWO

THE CURRENT SYSTEM

THE CONCEPT of paying workers according to their contribution is intrinsic to the American system of free enterprise. Indeed, for most members of the labor force, wages are determined by the rules of the marketplace. The most notable exception, the U.S. military establishment with its 2 million members, also happens to be the nation's largest employer. Unlike the pay systems governing most civilian workers, the armed forces' system is anchored to principles of institutionalism and paternalism. Rather than being paid strictly for work performed, members of the armed forces are paid according to their rank and seniority, and are entitled to a set of perquisites geared largely to meeting their "needs." These principles are embodied in the composition of military compensation.

What Constitutes Military Compensation?

The military compensation package consists of a wide assortment of pay, allowances, and benefits, the most important of which are displayed in table 2-1.[1] By convention, these elements are grouped into four categories: basic pay, quarters and subsistence allowances, and tax advantages, collectively called regular military compensation; special pays; fringe benefits; and other allowances.

1. A good deal of controversy surrounds the issue of military compensation. The military community is particularly sensitive about which items are included in the compensation package. Table 2-1 does not include all the elements that should be considered a part of military pay (a variety of veterans' benefits, for example), nor is there unanimous agreement that all the items shown should qualify as items of military pay (job-related expenses, for example). On balance, however, the data in table 2-1 provide a reasonable approximation of the cost incurred in compensating the military work force.

13

Table 2-1. Components of Military Pay, Allowances, and Benefits, and Their Costs, Fiscal 1978

Millions of dollars

Component	Cost
Regular military compensation	25,796
Basic pay	17,392
Quarters allowance (cash and in kind)	4,973
Subsistence allowance (cash and in kind)	1,931
Tax advantage (estimated)	1,500
Special pay	1,117
Enlistment and reenlistment bonuses	233
Sea duty	27
Medical officers	136
Incentive pay for hazardous duty	276
Miscellaneous	129
Separation pay	316
Supplemental benefits	13,489
Retirement pay	9,240
Medical care	2,771
Government contribution to social security	1,008
Commissary and exchange	428
Other	42
Other allowances	554
Total	40,956

Source: Adapted from *Report of the President's Commission on Military Compensation* (Government Printing Office, 1978), p. 9.

Regular Military Compensation

The centerpiece of the compensation system is basic pay.[2] It is the only cash element of military compensation to which every service member is entitled and which, like a civilian wage or salary, is considered to be "payment for work performed, responsibility assumed, or time worked."[3] Basic pay rates are tied to rank and accumulated years of military service. Effective October 1980, for example, annual pay ranged from $6,016 for a new recruit to $21,845 for an E-9 (the highest enlisted grade) with at least twenty-six years of service.[4] The schedule of basic pay rates provides

2. The term *basic pay* has been used since 1949; previously it was known as *base pay, pay of the troops,* or simply *pay*.

3. U.S. Department of Defense, Office of the Secretary of Defense, "Military Equivalent Salary," *The Third Quadrennial Review of Military Compensation: Staff Studies and Selected Supporting Papers,* vol. 1: *Regular Military Compensation* (DOD, 1976), p. 10.

4. See appendix table A-5 for basic pay rates of enlisted personnel as of October 1, 1980.

for automatic raises with increased service within each pay grade. To have pay raised beyond the maximum level in a pay grade requires governmentwide pay increases. Otherwise pay is increased through promotion to the next higher grade. The pay table is set up also to ensure that those in a lower grade will not earn more than those in a higher grade who have served the same number of years.

In addition to receiving basic pay, members of the armed services have traditionally been billeted and fed. Before World War II, lodging and meals were provided almost exclusively "in kind," but as U.S. standing forces grew larger and the family became a more prominent part of the military setting, this proved impractical. Today, only about one-half of all military personnel live in government quarters and even fewer—mostly unmarried junior personnel—receive subsistence in kind. In neither case does cash change hands; "free" goods and services are received.

Those who are not provided with meals or quarters, either because facilities are unavailable or because of individual preference, are paid cash allowances intended to defray the expense of obtaining the goods and services on the private economy. To offset food expenses, military personnel are provided cash "subsistence allowances" which in October 1980 amounted to about $83 a month for officers and about $120 a month for enlisted men.[5] Cash "quarters allowances," on the other hand, are based on rank and dependency status; they ranged from $103 a month for an unmarried recruit to $535 a month for a general officer with dependents.

Since subsistence and quarters allowances are not subject to federal income tax, military personnel enjoy a tax advantage. The magnitude of this saving—the equivalent of the additional cash income that would have to be provided to ensure the same take-home pay if allowances were taxable—in each case depends principally on the size of the allowances, total taxable income, and dependency status.

Taken together, basic pay, allowances, and the tax advantage constitute

---

5. Enlisted personnel draw larger allowances than officers because, before 1974, the rates were set under different procedures. Changes in subsistence allowances for officers had required specific legislation, and a monthly rate of $47.88 prevailed from 1952 to 1974. Enlisted personnel's allowances, which were pegged to the cost to the government of procuring food, lagged behind officers' allowances until the dramatic increase in food prices that occurred in 1973–74. The formula was changed in 1974, so that cash subsistence allowances for both officers and enlisted personnel increase by the same percentage. Enlisted personnel were receiving higher allowances than officers when the change was made, so their allowances continue to be higher.

Table 2-2. Value of Components of Regular Military Compensation for Enlisted Personnel, by Grade, 1978

Pay grade	Typical occupant			Regular military compensation (dollars)				
	Rank title[a]	Years of service	Number of dependents	Basic pay	Quarters allowance[b]	Subsistence allowance[b]	Average federal tax advantage	Total
E-9	Sergeant major	22	3	16,657	3,236	1,095	1,389	22,378
E-8	Master sergeant	18	3	13,536	2,992	1,095	1,105	18,727
E-7	Sergeant, first class	14	3	11,426	2,783	1,095	936	16,240
E-6	Staff sergeant	8	3	9,137	2,560	1,095	820	13,611
E-5	Sergeant	4	2	7,506	2,351	1,095	784	11,736
E-4	Corporal	3	1	6,772	2,070	1,095	625	10,562
E-3	Private, first class	less than 2	1	5,825	1,804	1,095	549	9,272
E-2	Private, PV-2	less than 2	0	5,609	1,098	1,095	481	8,283
E-1	Private, PV-1	less than 2	0	5,033	1,037	1,095	453	7,617

Source: Based on data provided by U.S. Department of Defense, Office of Assistant Secretary of Defense for Manpower, Reserve Affairs, and Logistics, October 1978. Annual rates effective October 1, 1978. Figures are rounded.

a. Army rank titles are shown here; titles vary by service.

b. Based on cash rates. For those receiving in-kind allowances, regular military compensation would differ from the totals shown here.

regular military compensation. Initially defined in the Military Pay Act of 1965, regular military compensation was established as the basis for linking military and civilian pay and for calculating comparability increases. Although it has not been used as an official measure since 1974, it is still widely regarded as the equivalent of a civilian salary.[6] Table 2-2 shows the amounts of regular military compensation for the typical enlisted person at each military grade as of October 1978, the latest date for which these data are available.

Special Pay

In addition to basic pay and allowances, military personnel may qualify for one or more forms of special pay. In the main, these payments are used for special purposes: to attract volunteers having particular expertise, to encourage the retention of workers with special skills, or to compensate for unusual risks or objectionable tasks.

Special pay is not unique to the military; civilian firms often pay a premium to overseas employees or to those in risky jobs. And the use of bonuses to attract and retain valuable personnel, perhaps most notably in professional sports, has become commonplace.

The use of special pay by the military is quite limited; in fiscal 1978, for example, such payments constituted less than 2 percent of the total military payroll.

Fringe Benefits

Supplementing pay and allowances, a variety of fringe benefits is included in the military compensation package. Among the most important are retirement and medical care.

Military personnel are entitled to retire after thirty to forty years of service, depending on the laws governing the particular service; at the

6. In 1974 the comparability formula was changed. In place of the provision that the percentage increase in federal white-collar civilian pay be applied to aggregate regular military compensation, Public Law 93-419 provided for the rate of increases to be applied equally to basic pay and to cash quarters and subsistence allowances. Subsequently Public Law 94-361 gave the President authority to deviate from the equal percentage provision when he determines such action to be in the nation's best interest. The amount allocated to basic pay may not be less than 75 percent of the amount that would have been allocated on an equal percentage basis. See 88 Stat. 1152 and 90 Stat. 925.

pleasure of the service secretary, however, an individual may retire after serving just twenty years. Those who retire at twenty years are entitled to 50 percent of their terminal basic pay. For each year beyond twenty, annuities increase at the rate of 2.5 percent of basic pay to a maximum of 75 percent. In addition, those found physically unfit for further service are granted physical disability retirements; the nature and amount of their benefits depend on the degree of disability. Retirement, then, is of no value to a person who does not serve long enough to acquire entitlement, but those who do (now about 8 percent of those who enlist) fall heir to one of the most generous retirement plans available. In fact, the typical military retiree can expect to collect more total pay during retirement than during active service.

Members of the armed forces are also entitled to unlimited health care. Their dependents can also receive medical care in military facilities. There is no charge for outpatient care, but when hospitalized, dependents of active-duty military personnel are charged $5.50 a day (the October 1980 rate). When military facilities are not available, dependent spouses and children are entitled to use civilian facilities, on a cost-sharing basis. For outpatient care the government pays 80 percent of allowable charges, beyond the first $50 a year for each dependent or $100 a year for a family with two or more dependents. For inpatient services the government pays all expenses except for a charge of $5.50 a day or $25, whichever is greater. The average cost of providing medical care is difficult to pin down, but it has been estimated at about $360 a year for each dependent.[7]

Other benefits available to military personnel include social security, unemployment compensation, and leave benefits, which are also available to most workers in the private sector, and commissaries and exchanges, and veterans' loans, bonuses, and preference in federal and state employment, which are not.

Other Allowances

Members of the armed forces are also entitled to allowances intended to defray special job-related expenses. These include the initial issue of,

7. Estimate in *Department of Defense Appropriation Bill, 1976*, S. Rept. 94-446, 94 Cong. 1 sess. (Government Printing Office, 1974), pp. 45–47, has been updated on the basis of the medical care component of the consumer price index to account for the effects of inflation.

or a cash allowance for, uniforms and clothing items and, for enlisted personnel, a monthly payment to maintain their wardrobe. And when assigned to areas outside the United States where the cost of living is deemed excessive or when assigned duties that require separation from their families for more than thirty days, personnel are entitled to additional allowances.

Setting Military Pay

Before 1967, adjustments in military pay were neither regular nor systematic. Separate legislation was needed for each change in basic pay, allowances, or benefits; legislators handled changes in an ad hoc fashion and increases were few and far between and then usually the result of intense lobbying or heightened international tensions. During the twenty-two years between the end of World War II and 1967, ten increases in basic pay were granted, quarters allowances were increased four times, and subsistence allowances were adjusted nine times—seven increases and two decreases. Of the ten increases in basic pay, four were across-the-board raises for all officers and enlisted personnel while the remaining six excluded personnel who had served less than two years.

In 1967 the principle of comparability was introduced into the military pay system. This principle, devised for federal civilian employees in 1962, provided a framework for establishing rates of pay for federal white-collar employees comparable to those of their counterparts in the private sector. The concept was extended to military personnel in 1967, mainly through the efforts of L. Mendel Rivers, chairman of the House Armed Services Committee. Rivers, wanting to ensure "that pay of our service personnel will continue its present relationship to that of their classified Federal contemporaries," sponsored legislation calling for automatic adjustments in military pay to match any increases in civilian pay.[8] Because of differences in the two pay systems, a special formula was devised for translating civilian pay increases into equivalent increases for the military. Initially, the equivalent of the total civilian increase was put into basic pay. Because of several anomalies that this created, a new formula was developed that provides for basic pay and cash allowances for quarters and subsistence to be increased by the same percentage as the

8. *Congressional Record,* vol. 113, pt. 22 (1967), pp. 30215-16.

increase in federal civilian pay; the secretary of defense is authorized, however, to redirect to quarters and subsistence allowances up to 25 percent of the total increase earmarked for basic pay.

Foundation and Rationale

While the military pay system differs in many respects from civilian systems, two dissimilarities are particularly conspicuous. The military pays its employees principally on the basis of rank and years of service while civilian employers, by emphasizing skill level and occupation, link pay more directly to work performed. In addition the military provides for the basic "necessities"; food, clothing, shelter, and medical care are furnished to all members of the armed forces and some entitlements are extended to their dependents.

The military compensation system is the legacy of the small, relatively unskilled, cadre-type forces that characterized the American armed services during most of their history before Pearl Harbor. Cash pay was extremely low, but practically everyone in the military, the large majority of whom were single, was provided free food, uniforms, and accommodations. Cash allowances were rare exceptions; thus, basic pay constituted the most visible yardstick of earnings. Since with few exceptions the rank and file were doing the same job—infantrymen and able-bodied seamen constituted the bulk of the armed forces—rank provided a reasonable measure of level of skill or proficiency and, by implication, of contribution. Even the relatively few who served in support jobs were first and foremost combat soldiers. Under these conditions, coupling pay to rank was internally consistent. And there was little emphasis on making comparisons with civilian pay systems, since most of the jobs in the armed forces were without a civilian parallel.

The rationale underlying the compensation system is found in the very nature of the U.S. armed forces; the military establishment is, in the idiom of the sociologist, an *institution* rather than an occupation. The distinction has been put vividly: "A civilian *works for* General Motors; but a career soldier *is in* the Army."[9]

---

9. U.S. Department of Defense, *Modernizing Military Pay,* vol. 1: *Active Duty Compensation,* Report of the First Quadrennial Review of Military Compensation (DOD, 1967), p. 101. Emphasis in original.

An institution, as perceived by a sociologist,

is legitimized in terms of values and norms, i.e., a purpose transcending individual self-interest in favor of a presumed higher good. Members of an institution are often viewed as following a calling; they generally regard themselves as being different or apart from the broader society and are so regarded by others. To the degree one's institutional membership is congruent with notions of self-sacrifice and dedication, it will usually enjoy esteem from the larger community. Although remuneration may not be comparable to what one might expect in the economy of the marketplace, this is often compensated for by an array of social benefits associated with an institutional format as well as psychic income. When grievances are felt, members of an institution do not organize themselves into interest groups. Rather, if redress is sought it takes the form of "one-on-one" recourse to superiors, with its implications of trust in the paternalism of the institution to take care of its own.[10]

The armed forces have quite clearly become anchored to such values and norms. Their institutional orientation seems an appropriate reflection of the many aspects of military employment that distinguish it from the normal run of civilian jobs. Military organizations with lines of authority and obligation between superior and subordinate that correspond closely with those of civilian organizations have traditionally been more disciplined and hierarchical. The core function of military forces—to engage in combat—requires that the individual respond immediately and without question to an order to put his life on the line; it demands a kind of discipline not generally associated with other occupational pursuits. The principle permeates the entire military establishment in a way that places the individual wholly at the disposal of the organization "which can decide what jobs he does, how and when he does them, what hours he works and the conditions in which he works and lives, entirely without consultation with the employee."[11]

How to motivate individuals to make such an "unlimited commitment" and to foster the sense of dedication considered crucial to the effectiveness of military forces, particularly those engaged in combat, has long been a vexing question. Traditionally, money has not been the only answer; service to the country has been encouraged largely as a sacrifice to be made out of patriotism or a sense of moral indebtedness. Thus military leaders have gone to great lengths to create a professional identity—literally a

10. Charles C. Moskos, Jr., "From Institution to Occupation: Trends in Military Organization," *Armed Forces and Society*, vol. 4 (Fall 1977), p. 42.

11. United Kingdom, National Board for Prices and Incomes, *Standing Reference on the Pay of the Armed Forces: Second Report*, Report 116, Cmnd. 4079 (Her Majesty's Stationery Office, 1969), p. 6.

different way of life in which cohesion, unity of purpose, and reciprocal loyalty are emphasized.[12]

To promote this unity and bonding, characteristics common to all members that distinguish them from the rest of society are emphasized. It is not surprising, then, that the military pay system has been tailored to serve that model.

The services' practice of providing the troops with basic necessities evolved during a period when the military unit was, in effect, a home for the vast majority of the rank and file. These paternalistic provisions have endured, even in the face of the contemporary military's family-oriented setting, largely to sustain the "special character of military life." Today some 3 million dependents of military personnel are eligible for a wide range of benefits generally not provided by employers in the nonmilitary sector. Indeed, the military's pay and allowance system, in which a large fraction of total compensation depends on the worker's family size, may be unique in American society.

Differences among personnel that are not necessary to sustain the profession's own value system are played down, and the equal value of all individuals to the total effort is stressed. Just how seriously the armed forces take this concept is illustrated by their response to the "responsibility pay" authorized in the Military Pay Act of 1958. On its own initiative the Senate Armed Services Committee amended the act to provide additional pay for officers in certain positions in recognition of their greater responsibilities. The committee believed this additional pay was justified because:

(1) Under the present pay system, an officer's pay is determined principally by his rank. It is recognized that both the abilities and responsibilities of officers within a particular grade vary to a considerable degree.

(2) The changing nature and complexity of our weapons systems are creating demands for unusual responsibility in both staff and command assignments, or a combination of both. These responsibilities, in many cases, may be distinguishable from the bulk of others held by those in that rank.[13]

The military, after ignoring the provision for five years, sought unsuccessfully to have it repealed in the Uniformed Services Pay Act of 1963. They argued that "there should be no distinction between persons

---

12. *Active Duty Compensation*, p. 101.

13. *Adjusting the Method of Computing Basic Pay for Officers and Enlisted Members of the Uniformed Services to Provide Proficiency Pay for Enlisted Members thereof and for Other Purposes*, S. Rept. 85-1472, 85 Cong. 2 sess. (GPO, 1958), pp. 7–8.

of equal rank and length of service for the purpose of pay since rank itself should be considered equal with responsibility." Moreover, the provision "would be difficult to administer without serious problems of equity and morale."[14]

IN THIS institutional setting, which military service one is a member of transcends which job one fills. "The organization one belongs to creates the feeling of shared interest, not the other way around . . . the sense of community in the military thus runs up and down, not sideways across— religiously, racially, as well as occupationally—as in civilian society."[15] This concept is reflected particularly in the existence of a pay table that entitles everyone of the same rank who has served the same number of years to the same amount of basic pay, whether infantryman, radar mechanic, or clerk. Implicit is the notion that all are making equal contributions to national defense.

14. *Military Pay Increase,* S. Rept. 88-387, 88 Cong. 1 sess. (GPO, 1963), pp. 29–30. The provision was used on a limited basis to compensate some officers serving as province or riverine force advisers in Vietnam. In 1980 the Navy authorized responsibility pay to ship captains, aviation squadron commanders, and some unit commanding officers. The Army, however, in continuing its opposition to the concept, maintained that "the use of monetary compensation as an incentive for assumption of command responsibilities runs counter to the Army's fundamental belief that command is a privilege limited to a few officers and is a reward in and of itself." *Army Times,* March 31, 1980.

15. Charles C. Moskos, Jr., "The Enlisted Ranks in the All-Volunteer Army," in John B. Keeley, ed., *The All-Volunteer Force and American Society* (University Press of Virginia, 1978), p. 56.

CHAPTER THREE

FLAWS IN THE SYSTEM

IN LARGE PART the uniqueness of the military pay system can be attributed to the nature of personnel management in the armed forces. The military services operate what is perhaps the most visible and largest of closed personnel systems; all workers are hired at the entry level, at the bottom of a hierarchical pyramid, and vacancies are normally filled internally by promotions. In most civilian personnel management systems, workers may enter laterally in jobs and at pay levels commensurate with their qualifications and previous work experience. In open systems, pay relationships and manpower conditions usually interact at every job and skill level; adjustments in pay differentials may affect only a few workers; and temporary manpower imbalances in one part of the system need not have widespread consequences for the system as a whole.

Open or closed, personnel and compensation systems are typically operated to attain more than the immediate goal of managing manpower. To be viable, they cannot ignore efficiency considerations. Indeed, in private organizations, where running a profitable business is an overriding objective, efficiency criteria are stringently applied. But even in the government, where profit-making is not a factor, efficiency in the salary structure is important if public service is to be performed by competent people and at reasonable cost.[1] The nature of their mission makes competence especially important for the armed forces.

---

1. Clearly not all markets are the same, just as not all employers' manpower needs and nature of output are the same. Moreover, the market-clearing mechanism is often influenced by administrative, institutional, and political forces and other noneconomic factors. Nonetheless, market systems usually behave quite predictably; changes in pay levels are normally accompanied by changes in employment, and vice versa. It is not unlikely that these considerations have played a role in the setting of government employees' salaries. The federal government uses three statutory pay systems for its white-collar labor force alone: the general schedule, the foreign

Table 3-1. Index of Estimated Average Annual Wage or Salary Earnings of Full-time Civilian Workers, by Occupational Category, 1978

Clerical category = 100

Occupational category	Earnings index
All professional and technical	164
Professional and technical excluding engineers and physicians	159
Engineering technicians	143
Health technologists and technicians	127
Other	174
Clerical	100
Craft	147
Service (except private household)	88
Protective service	132

Source: Based on data provided by U.S. Department of Labor, Bureau of Labor Statistics, January 1979, on usual weekly wage or salary earnings of civilian workers employed full time (35 hours per week or more).

Distortions in Occupational Pay Differentials

The fact that workers' pay varies depending on the nature of the work performed is taken for granted by most people, whether they have ever held a job or not. To be sure, some jobs have always paid better than others. Significant differences have long distinguished the earnings of plumbers or electricians from the earnings of clerks or cooks in civilian employment; among male, full-time, full-year workers, for example, those in professional and technical occupations earn an average of about 55 percent more than unskilled workers.[2]

Regardless of the theories that may be used to explain, sometimes to legitimize, and not infrequently to rationalize the functions of occupational pay differentials in the civilian economy, those differentials have important effects on the military work force: the armed services must seek

service system, and a system for certain employees in the Department of Medicine and Surgery in the Veterans' Administration. See U.S. Civil Service Commission, Bureau of Personnel Management Information Systems, *Pay Structure of the Federal Civil Service,* Federal Civilian Workforce Statistics, SM 33-77 (Government Printing Office, 1979), pp. 1–2, 17. It also uses the executive schedule (for top government officials) and the federal wage system (for employees in blue-collar occupations) as well as a number of systems that are administratively determined.

2. See U.S. Bureau of the Census, *Census of Population, 1970,* Subject Reports: *Occupational Characteristics,* Final Report PC(2)-7A (GPO, 1973), table 1.

qualified volunteers in the civilian sector and they must compete with that sector to retain those whom they have already trained.

The armed forces' task is doubly difficult because of the myriad of occupations and specialties that exist in the modern military and because the range of jobs and pay packages in the civilian economy is so wide.

Differentials in the Civilian Work Force

Wage differentials in the civilian sector are significant, as table 3-1 shows. Indexes of the average annual wage or salary earning of full-time civilian workers (based on the mean earnings of clerical workers) indicate that technical workers, excluding engineers and physicians, earn, on average, 59 percent more than clerical workers.[3] Engineering technicians' earnings are 43 percent higher and those of health technologists and technicians 27 percent higher than those of clerical workers; both occupations have distinct counterparts (and a high concentration of workers) in the military. Even more favored are craftsmen. And while the earnings of service workers are the most depressed, those in protective services (notably policemen, detectives, and firemen, as well as less-well-paid crossing guards, bridge tenders, and watchmen) earn, on average, 32 percent more than the typical clerk does.[4]

Differentials in the Military Work Force

The military pay structure yields no such contrasts. Not only is a single basic pay schedule used for personnel in all the services, but it

---

3. Civilian compensation consists of both pay in connection with work performed and benefits payments (including in-kind benefits). The Bureau of Labor Statistics defines the gross payroll as "pay for working time, pay for vacations, holidays, sick leave, and civic and personal leave; severance pay; and non-production bonuses." Benefits or supplements "include all employer expenditures for compensation other than wages and salaries. They consist of expenditures for retirement programs . . . ; expenditures for life insurance and health benefit programs (except sick leave); expenditures for unemployment benefit programs (except severance pay); payments to vacation and holiday funds; and payments to savings and thrift plans." U.S. Department of Labor Statistics, *Employee Compensation in the Private Nonfarm Economy,* Bulletin 1770 (GPO, 1973), table A-1, p. 17. Since there are no official definitions reconciling the significant differences between the military and civilian pay systems, comparisons in this chapter are based on regular military compensation and wage or salary payments in the civilian sector.

4. Bureau of the Census, *Occupational Characteristics*, table 1.

Table 3-2. Average Annual Regular Military Compensation of Enlisted Personnel, by Occupational Category, 1978

Occupational category	Regular military compensation	
	Dollars	*Index (clerical category = 100)*
Technical	9,804	96
Electronic equipment repairmen	10,175	100
Communications and intelligence specialists	9,574	94
Medical and dental specialists	9,574	94
Other technical and allied specialists	9,874	97
Clerical	10,175	100
Craft	9,448	93
Electrical and mechanical equipment repairmen	9,423	93
Other craftsmen	9,574	94
Other	9,087	89
General military skills, including ground combat[a]	8,972	88
Service and supply handlers	9,273	91

Sources: Based on U.S. Department of Defense, Office of Assistant Secretary of Defense for Manpower, Reserve Affairs, and Logistics, *Manpower Requirements Report for FY 1979* (DOD, 1978), table 13, p. xiv-41, and data provided by the office.

a. Officially entitled "infantry, gun crews, and seamanship specialists."

applies to all occupations or individual specialties. Rates of pay are set to correspond to nine pay grades; they vary with longevity in the service but not by occupation. The nearly total absence of occupational differentials is by far the most striking feature of the military pay structure.

The regular military compensation of enlisted personnel, whether in the more technical occupational categories, or the clerical area, or service and supply, varies little, as shown in table 3-2.[5] The index of average earnings, based on the average earnings of clerical personnel, falls between 93 and 100 for most occupational categories, and falls below 90 only for general military skills. In the individual services the variation in

5. The shape of the pay structure depends, of course, on pay rates and on the grade distribution of personnel. Since little official data on the military pay structure exist, estimating average pay by military occupation is a task in and by itself. Data do exist on rates of regular military compensation (basic pay, quarters and subsistence allowances, and the tax advantage which accrues because allowances are not taxed), which all military personnel receive, and on the grade distribution of enlisted personnel, all of whom can be assumed to be engaged in full-time, full-year work. Focusing on regular military compensation (which is widely used to denote military salary) excludes special, incentive, and separation pays, but these pays account for only 2 percent of the total military compensation.

Table 3-3. Index of Average Annual Regular Military Compensation of Enlisted Personnel, by Occupational Category and by Service, 1978

Clerical category = 100

Occupational category	Army	Navy	Marine Corps	Air Force
Technical	95	97	95	97
Clerical	100	100	100	100
Craft	89	95	93	93
Other	89	97	87	92
General military skills, including ground combat[a]	89	100	86	92
Service and supply handlers	91	95	89	92

Sources: Same as table 3-2.
a. Officially entitled "infantry, gun crews, and seamanship specialists."

military earnings by occupational area is also minimal, as table 3-3 illustrates.[6]

All of this might be expected as a natural outcome of a pay system that views all tasks as equally important and those who perform them as equally productive. But that assumption must be challenged. The military in effect fails to recognize that some jobs are perceived as being less attractive, more difficult, less demanding, or simply better or worse than others; some may actually be better or worse than others. The armed forces, by offering equal pay for unequal jobs, assign as prominent a role to, say, the enlisted clerk as to the combat soldier; yet recruitment for combat-related positions has always been more difficult.[7] And their failure to offer pay differentials to enlisted technicians and craftsmen is inconsistent with the services' growing needs for these specialists.[8] All in all, it is likely that

6. The reenlistment bonuses that enlisted personnel are eligible for at the end of their first or second term of service go to relatively few persons and are so small that they have practically no effect on the structure of military pay. In fiscal 1978, bonuses averaging $1,233 were paid to 12,596 of the 432,614 enlisted personnel in technical jobs, bonuses averaging $230 to 854 of the 266,511 in clerical jobs, bonuses averaging $1,012 to 9,062 of the 426,749 in craft jobs, bonuses averaging $660 to 13,343 of the 260,087 in combat jobs, and bonuses averaging $627 to 4,819 of the 160,760 in service and supply jobs. Based on data provided by Office of Assistant Secretary of Defense for Manpower, Reserve Affairs, and Logistics, 1979.

7. Even though the proportion of military personnel engaged in combat-related tasks has decreased significantly over the past quarter-century, it is surprising that in the Army and the Marine Corps—the services that need and rely on the combat soldier most—the internal structure of pay favors the combat soldier least.

8. The absence of pay differentials for these specialists is also inconsistent with the fact that outside employment opportunities are much greater for them than for enlisted clerks.

because of the military pay system and its by-product—the pay structure —the Army and to a lesser extent the Marine Corps are having trouble attracting recruits for combat jobs while for the Air Force and Navy the "hemorrhage of talent" is alarming.[9]

Transplanting the occupational pay differentials prevailing in the civilian sector to the military would, of course, be neither feasible nor appropriate. The relative lack of dispersion in military earnings is due, in part, to special factors. Armed forces personnel are not as likely as their civilian counterparts to suffer unemployment spells which disrupt their earnings pattern and may reduce the rate of growth of their personal earnings; as a result, average regular military compensation would probably need to vary less across the occupational spectrum than civilian wages and salaries. Also, because the military work force is more homogeneous than the civilian sector force in terms of educational attainment, earnings dispersion would tend to be less pronounced in the armed forces. Yet even when these factors are taken into consideration, the military's slight differentials in occupational pay are markedly out of phase with those in the rest of the economy.[10]

Although perfect comparability does not exist between military and civilian occupations, it is reasonable to examine the overall comparability of the two sectors by broad occupational categories. While there may be a greater variety of jobs for craftsmen, for instance, in the civilian sector, so long as task variety and content are generally similar, it is possible to compare military and civilian employment and earnings in the craft occupational category. Moreover, some data can be disaggregated, so that it is possible to compare civilian occupations with their direct counterparts in the military.

Generally, service occupations are comparable in the military and civilian sectors. Combat is an important exception; because it is a truly unique profession, employment and earnings data on combat positions are shown separately in tables 3-2 and 3-3. Some combat specialties, however, clearly fall within the conventional limits of service jobs; installation

9. U.S. Department of the Navy, Office of Information, "A Matter of Priority," *Navy Policy Briefs*, February 1980, p. 4.

10. For example, the index of earnings of employed civilian male high school graduates aged 25–34 where clerical workers = 100 is 122 for professional and technical workers, 115 for craftsmen, and 97 for service workers. Bureau of the Census, *Census of Population, 1970*, Subject Report: *Earnings by Occupation and Education*, Final Report PC (2)-8B (GPO, 1973), table 1.

security, for instance, "includes specialists who guard weapon systems, defend installations, and protect personnel, equipment, and facilities."[11]

One other highly significant difference between the military and civilian work forces is their age composition. About one-third of the civilian workers represented in the civilian earnings data in table 3-1 are over the age of forty-four, whereas the proportion of enlisted personnel in that age group is negligible. In order to compare military data to data on the earnings of civilian workers by age as well as by occupational category, it is necessary to turn to a segment of the civilian work force—the nonmilitary employees of the Department of Defense—whose earnings data are broken down by age.

Differentials in the Defense Department's Civilian Work Force

Of some 940,000 civilian employees of the Department of Defense, about 722,000 work in what are classified as enlisted level occupations; these are grouped by the Department of Defense into the same number and type of occupational categories used to classify the jobs of enlisted personnel. As a result, occupational categories of civilians and military personnel, at the enlisted level, are directly comparable.[12] Moreover, it is possible to exclude earnings data on full-time civilian workers aged forty-five and over, thus making the military and civilian earnings data directly comparable (with the qualification that regular military compensation is compared with wage or salary earnings).

The disparities in wage and salary earnings in civilian positions are shown in table 3-4 (the general schedule, for white-collar workers, includes all of the clerical occupations and the vast majority of technical jobs, while the federal wage system, for blue-collar workers, covers electronics equipment repairmen and most other occupations). The index variations make clear the significant differences in earnings by occupational category that exist among civilian workers employed by the Department of Defense. Earnings of craftsmen far exceed those of workers in all other categories, followed by the earnings of technical workers. It is particularly interesting that clerical workers receive the lowest mean salary, in relative terms. By contrast to the pay differences of military per-

11. U.S. Department of Defense, Office of Assistant Secretary of Defense for Manpower, Reserve Affairs, and Logistics, *Occupational Conversion Manual: Enlisted/Officer/Civilian* (DOD, 1977), p. 1.

12. Comparable military and civilian occupations within the Department of Defense are described in detail in ibid.

Table 3-4. Index of Average Annual Wage or Salary Earnings of Full-time Civilian Employees Aged 17–44 of the Department of Defense, by Occupational Category, 1978
Clerical category = 100

Occupational category	Earnings index
Technical	134
Electronic equipment repairmen	162
Other	118
Clerical	100
Craft	152
Electrical and mechanical equipment repairmen	153
Other craftsmen	151
Other	117
General military skills, including ground combat[a]	104
Service and supply handlers	120

Source: Based on data provided by Office of Assistant Secretary of Defense for Manpower, Reserve Affairs, and Logistics, 1979.
a. Officially entitled "infantry, gun crews, and seamanship specialists."

sonnel shown in table 3-2, civilians working in service and supply jobs in the Defense Department as well as those few assigned to combat-related duties receive salaries that, on average, exceed those of clerical personnel by 20 percent and 4 percent, respectively. The earnings of civilian personnel in the Department of Defense, like those of all civilian workers, vary significantly and consistently by occupational area.[13]

Training Costs

Implicit in the military pay relationships (table 3-1) is the notion that, be it a traditional military task, office work, repair or maintenance of equipment, the cost of having a task completed does not vary. The relative training costs in the different occupational categories of the enlisted force run contrary to that notion.

The value of any worker's contribution depends in large part on training, both formal and on the job.[14] Other things being equal, the more

13. Sex discrimination probably played a significant role in depressing the earnings of civilian clerical workers—including those in the Defense Department—since these workers are mostly women. But even among young male workers, those working in clerical jobs earn on average only 3 percent more than the least well paid (service workers). Moreover, even in this all-male group of workers, the earnings of technicians and craftsmen are considerably higher than those of clerical personnel.

14. See, for example, H. S. Houthakker, "Education and Income," *Review of Economics and Statistics,* vol. 41 (February 1959), pp. 24–28; Giora Hanoch, "An Economic Analysis of Earnings and Schooling," *Journal of Human Resources,* vol. 2 (Summer 1967), pp. 310–29.

Table 3-5. Length of Initial Training Courses for Enlisted Personnel, by Service, Fiscal 1978

Number of days

Service and course	Length of course
Army	
Law enforcement specialist	56
Light weapons infantryman	56
Nuclear power plant operator	365
Navy	
Apprentice (seaman, fireman, etc.)	16
Basic submarine training	45
Marine Corps	
Basic administrative clerk	20
Infantryman	44
Basic electronics specialist	122
Air Force	
Security specialist	37
Inventory management specialist	44
Avionics aerospace ground equipment specialist	354

Source: U.S. Department of Defense, Office of Assistant Secretary of Defense for Manpower and Reserve Affairs, *Military Manpower Training Report for FY 1978: and Report on Efficiency and Effectiveness of Military Training* (DOD, 1977), p. v-5.

training workers receive and hence the greater the training investment becomes, the better their job performance and the higher their earnings are expected to be. Investment in personnel training in the armed forces, as in the civilian sector, varies significantly by occupational area, both among and within the services. Courses taught to prepare enlisted individuals for work in the technical occupations (for example, nuclear power plant operation, basic electronics, and repair and operation of avionics aerospace ground equipment) last much longer than other courses, naturally pushing the cost of technical training upward. Clerical personnel, as table 3-5 shows, can be trained in a much shorter time and at a lower cost.

Though estimates of training costs are not routinely available, the results of a special study of the cost of providing training to naval personnel suggest how wide the variations can be.[15] Training in the crafts lasts longer and costs considerably more than the training of personnel in other occupational areas, as table 3-6 shows. While evidence from such a small

15. See Robert Shishko, *The Economics of Naval Ship Automation: An Analysis of Proposed Automation of the DE-1052,* R-1790-ARPA, prepared for Advanced Research Projects Agency, U.S. Department of Defense (Santa Monica, Calif.: Rand Corp., 1975).

Table 3-6. Duration and Cost of Training for Navy Enlisted Personnel, 1974

Occupational category and rank title	Duration (years)	Cost (dollars)[a]
Craft		
Interior communications electrician	1.35	12,399.90
Machinist's mate	1.27	11,014.20
Boiler technician	1.27	10,944.90
Engineerman	1.27	10,893.40
Clerical		
Storekeeper	1.08	9,120.50
Yeoman	0.81	7,468.00
Boatswain's mate	0.87	7,075.30
Signalman	0.91	7,906.80
Quartermaster	0.79	6,917.70

Source: Robert Shishko, *The Economics of Naval Ship Automation: An Analysis of Proposed Automation of the DE-1052*, R-1790-ARPA, prepared for Advanced Research Projects Agency, U.S. Department of Defense (Santa Monica, Calif.: Rand Corp., 1975), table B-2, p. 62.
a. Undiscounted fiscal 1974 dollars.

occupational sample is of limited utility, it at least suggests that the occupational earnings of enlisted personnel are out of line with the value of their contribution as measured by training investment.[16]

Other Structural Rigidities

The military pay structure appears to be seriously short on efficiency and consequently on effectiveness in promoting the adequate staffing of military occupations. While the Department of Defense in order to fill some 1 million nonmilitary positions with qualified personnel is compelled to pay civilian workers on the basis of their occupation, it expects and is expected to man roughly 1.8 million enlisted military positions on an entirely different basis. Military pay policy, characterized by the conspicuous absence of occupational wage differentials, stresses reward for time in service, across the board and without much distinction for occupational specialty.

16. If the nature of military training is such that the resulting skills are "specific" —not easily, if at all, transferable to the civilian sector—then the services presumably need not stress financial incentives to retain personnel. The pattern of retention rates (see chap. 4) suggests that highly trained enlisted specialists can with little difficulty apply their expertise to civilian jobs.

Table 3-7. Index of Average Regular Military Compensation of Enlisted Personnel, by Age and Occupational Category, 1978

Clerical category = 100

	Age			
Occupational category	*18–24 (clerical = $8,955[a])*	*25–34 (clerical = $11,903[a])*	*35–44 (clerical = $13,471[a])*	*45 and above (clerical = $19,608[a])*
Technical	100	102	104	96
Clerical	100	100	100	100
Craft	99	98	96	93
Other	99	93	104	91
General military skills, including ground combat[b]	99	91	108	91
Service and supply	98	93	94	91

Sources: Same as table 3-2.
a. Average regular military compensation of clerical workers.
b. Officially entitled "infantry, gun crews, and seamanship specialists."

Longevity

Job tenure—the length of time an individual is employed—is an important determinant of pay, and compensation generally, in almost all pay systems. In the military it is the most critical variable in the pay equation: rates of military pay are expressly and automatically tied to longevity in the service, or job tenure—or, in still other words, seniority. Thus, while an enlisted person's occupation has practically no consequences for his earnings, how long he has served in the armed forces does. For example, maximum regular military compensation at the E-5 grade level is (at 1977 pay rates) $2,747, or 28 percent, above the minimum ($9,705); similarly, at the E-7 level maximum compensation is $5,657, or 44 percent, above the minimum ($12,906).[17] Pay raises are awarded automatically, as longevity increases, and thus cannot be viewed as related to merit. In the absence of occupational differentials, military pay turns out to be principally a function of length of service and, by necessity, of age.

Table 3-7 highlights the direct relationship between job tenure and earnings in the military and the fact that the underlying pay structure is practically unaffected by tenure or, by analogy, experience acquired in the

17. Derived from data in U.S. Department of Defense, Office of the Assistant Secretary of Defense for Manpower, Reserve Affairs, and Logistics, *Manpower Requirements Report for FY 1979* (DOD, 1978), table 13, p. xiv-41.

Table 3-8. Index of Average Wage or Salary Earnings of Full-time Civilian Employees of the Department of Defense, by Age and Occupational Category, 1978

Clerical category = 100

	Age			
Occupational category	*18–24* *(clerical =* *$8,859[a])*	*25–34* *(clerical =* *$10,193[a])*	*35–44* *(clerical =* *$12,305[a])*	*45 and above* *(clerical =* *$13,486[a])*
Technical	115	127	133	129
Clerical	100	100	100	100
Craft	159	150	143	134
Other	126	118	115	110
General military skills, including ground combat	113	102	103	98
Service and supply	127	119	116	111

Source: Based on data provided by Office of Assistant Secretary of Defense for Manpower, Reserve Affairs, and Logistics, 1979.

a. Average earnings of clerical workers.

enlisted work force. For example, enlisted craftsmen remain relatively underpaid in all age groups; their earnings are 98 percent of clerical earnings in the twenty-five to thirty-four age group and fall to 93 percent in the oldest age group.

While it is conceivable that entry-level pay might not vary by occupation when an employer bears the full cost of all subsequent training, it is difficult to envision a pay system that treats seasoned workers as if there were practically no differences in the value of their services.

When the average wage or salary earnings of full-time civilians employed by the Defense Department are recast by age and major occupational category, the inequities in the earnings profiles of the military are obvious. Table 3-8 illustrates that even though age and working experience of civilian employees are related to earnings, so is occupation. Among the youngest of civilian workers employed by the Department of Defense, wide earning differentials can be observed. And, while these tend to become less pronounced among the oldest of workers, they always remain significantly greater than is the case in the military.

Finally, as table 3-9 indicates, the gap in the relative pay patterns of military and civilian personnel in the Defense Department's enlisted-level job categories tends to narrow at the point when, for all practical purposes, the armed forces have least to worry about the competition (the thirty-five through forty-four age group). Whether the gap is appropriate at the youngest age group is an open question—regular military compen-

Table 3-9. Ratio of Military to Civilian Workers' Earnings, by Age and Occupational Category, 1978[a]

	Age			
Occupational category	*18–24*	*25–34*	*35–44*	*45 and over*
Technical	0.88	0.88	0.86	1.08
Clerical	1.01	1.10	1.09	1.45
Craft	0.63	0.72	0.73	1.01
Other	0.80	0.90	0.99	1.21
General military skills, including ground combat	0.87	0.99	0.99	1.36
Service and supply	0.76	0.89	0.98	1.20

Sources: Tables 3-7 and 3-8.

a. A ratio of less than 1.00 indicates that regular military compensation is less than civilian workers' earnings, and a ratio of more than 1.00 that it is more.

sation is a much smaller percentage of total compensation than the wages and salaries of civilian workers are, and enlistment offers special advantages to inexperienced workers. But, given the relative differences in pay at the entry level and the absence of differentials by occupation in the armed forces, the earnings of all but the youngest group of enlisted personnel seem seriously unbalanced. Junior clerical personnel receive typically about as much in regular military compensation as their civilian counterparts receive in total earnings, 13 percent more at the ages of thirty-five through forty-four, and 45 percent more at the ages of forty-five and over. By contrast, focusing on absolute levels of earnings, the regular military compensation of enlisted craftsmen at ages eighteen through twenty-four is 37 percent less than that of their defense civilian counterparts, and 36 percent less at ages thirty-five through forty-four. Only in the small group of the most senior enlisted craftsmen does the average regular military compensation approach the earnings of civilians in the Defense Department.

Comparability and Its Anomalies

Increases in military pay levels based on longevity operate within the framework of pay tables in effect during a particular year. But the problems that the tenure system creates are exacerbated by yet another mechanism—equally automatic, arbitrary, and across the board—which provides for changes in the pay tables themselves. The measure that in 1967 extended to the military the comparability to private wage levels awarded to civil servants in 1962 provided for automatic increases in military pay.[18] Percentage increases equivalent to those awarded civilian employees were to be applied equally to all pay grades, in all occupations and in all of the services. The level of military pay was not to be initially subjected to comparison with federal pay or, directly or indirectly, with private sector pay. Under the procedure that was instituted, military pay increases were awarded automatically and irrespective of manning conditions.[19]

Military pay raises have never been contingent on the establishment of comparability with civilian jobs, work levels, and pay rates. It thus seems unlikely that the comparability mechanism could be expected to align pay levels with manpower requirements in the armed forces. Indeed, whether the pay increases have been sufficient, warranted, dictated by, or in any way related to military personnel requirements are not questions that the comparability procedure addresses.[20] If, as the evidence suggests, federal pay increases under the comparability principle have not been appropriately allocated among civilian employees,[21] it would be reasonable to expect that the adverse consequences would be even greater in the military sector.

Extension of the comparability principle to the military labor force has raised pay levels generally. But this in no way deals with pay levels that were already too low or too high. More than anything else, institutionalization of the comparability procedure has contributed to isolating the issues of manpower conditions and pay levels from one another. The Defense Manpower Commission in 1976 concluded that disregard for manpower supply conditions was the most serious defect of the comparability principle for civilian compensation.

18. For a fuller discussion of the rationale, implementation, and consequences of the "prevailing wage principle," see Walter Fogel and David Lewin, "Wage Determination in the Public Sector," *Industrial and Labor Relations Review,* vol. 27 (April 1974), pp. 410–31.

19. See chap. 2. Subsequent military pay raises through fiscal 1980 have been on a par with federal pay increases. For employees under the general schedule, the Bureau of Labor Statistics conducts an annual survey of professional, administrative, technical, and clerical pay (the PATC survey) whose results are used in aligning pay rates with those prevailing in private industry.

20. The same, of course, holds true for the federal civilian work force. In fact, many of the comments here are relevant to the process for determining federal civilian pay.

21. For presentation of such evidence and a critique of the workings of the comparability process, see Sharon P. Smith, *Equal Pay in the Public Sector: Fact or Fantasy,* Research Report 122 (Industrial Relations Section, Department of Economics, Princeton University, 1977).

This defect in the principle applies with even greater force to the military. The principal items of military compensation are increased across the board by the average increase in Civil Service salaries. There is no pretense that military jobs are comparable to either private sector or Civil Service jobs. Adjustments occur with no reference to military recruitment and retention experience. . . . The Department of Defense has no role in the annual adjustment of the major components of military compensation or in Federal civilian compensation, although it is by far the largest employer of Federal civilians.[22]

And in 1978 the President's Commission on Military Compensation charged that the comparability increases do "little to make military wage rates more competitive."

The automatic annual adjustment of the [compensation] levels of all personnel, without regard to manning problems, does little to introduce efficiency into the system.

The policy of equal percentage across-the-board annual pay raises precludes the use of these raises to adjust the pay schedule to meet manning shortages or overages.[23]

In effect, pay adjustments that are deemed necessary for a federal white-collar labor force whose median age is about forty-five are automatically being applied to a military work force that is roughly 55 percent blue-collar and whose median age is about twenty-four.

Both the mechanism by which military pay rates are increased and the cumulative impact of pay raises push the Defense Department's payroll in only one direction—up. In and by itself, this phenomenon should not be viewed as peculiar in an economy characterized by annual increases in nominal pay levels. But it could be viewed as accounting, at least in part, for the paradox of manpower imbalances in the midst of higher pay rates in the armed forces.

The Consequences

For too long, the military pay system has remained so rigidly structured that one of the fundamental goals it is supposed to serve stands unmet—and, in some important ways, compromised.

Important as the doctrinal, ideological, or, more generally, institutional

22. Defense Manpower Commission, *Defense Manpower; The Keystone of National Security,* Report to the President and Congress, April 1976 (GPO, 1976), p. 283.

23. *Report of the President's Commission on Military Compensation* (GPO, 1978), pp. 125–27.

role of military pay may have been considered, its allocative function has been consistently pointed out: military pay has always been viewed as a critical determinant of the number and quality of personnel in the armed forces. The first official articulation of this principle after World War II was explicit. In his request in 1948 for a comprehensive study of the military pay system, Secretary of Defense James V. Forrestal asked his Advisory Commission on Service Pay to consider that "in the first place, the Services need a system of compensation which will enable them to *attract* and *retain* their fair share of the best kind of men for all the many varieties of jobs in the several Services."[24] Almost ten years later, at the request of yet another secretary of defense, the U.S. Defense Advisory Committee on Professional and Technical Compensation presented its recommendations for a program of compensation that would "make it possible [for the services] to *attract, retain* and motivate [personnel with] skills required by the Department of Defense today and in the future."[25] And in 1967 the Pentagon panel that conducted the first quadrennial review of military compensation also was guided by the objective that the military pay system should be *"attracting, retaining* and motivating to career service the kinds and numbers of people our uniformed services need."[26]

These goals may seem self-evident. Even during periods of conscription, the compensation principles enunciated by decisionmakers and policy planners were based on job skills. These principles are even more relevant in an environment where the armed forces are expected to meet the competition. Yet they have not been actually embodied in recent military pay policies; as matters stand, the competition has not been met, and chances are that it will remain unmet as long as military pay remains unresponsive to market conditions. By not recognizing the differences in the value of occupational qualifications—differences that civilian pay systems have always emphasized—military pay becomes especially attractive to personnel possessing the less valuable skills, while it fails to satisfy those possessing the more valuable skills; as a result, the armed forces end up

24. U.S. Advisory Commission on Service Pay, *Career Compensation for the Uniformed Services,* vol. 1: *Report and Recommendation for the Secretary of Defense* (GPO, 1948), p. vii. Emphasis added.

25. *Report of the Defense Advisory Committee on Professional and Technical Compensation,* vol. 1: *Military Personnel* (GPO, 1957), p. vii. Emphasis added.

26. U.S. Department of Defense, *Modernizing Military Pay,* vol. 1: *Active Duty Compensation,* Report of the First Quadrennial Review of Military Compensation (DOD, 1967), p. xiv. Emphasis added.

paying some of their workers more than they need to and others less than they ought to.

And if history is a reliable guide, growth in the military payroll in itself cannot be expected to redress the imbalance. Indeed, over the past decade or so, expenditures on military manpower have risen significantly. For fiscal 1981 the Department of Defense earmarked about $30 billion for pay and allowances of just over 2 million active duty troops; in fiscal 1968 about $19 billion was paid to 3.5 million service members.[27] The per capita increase in military payroll costs over the period was close to threefold. Much of the increase can be laid at the doorstep of inflation, and some portion reflects the transfer to the defense budget of the implicit conscription tax borne by draftees.[28] Whatever its cause, the pattern of rising expenditures appears to have done little to enrich the experience mix of the armed forces and, indeed, it may have contributed to the exodus of skilled personnel.

The problem is not new. In 1967 a study conducted as part of the first quadrennial review revealed that while each service could "meet its total active duty enlisted requirements in 1965 . . . there was a consistent pattern of experience imbalances. . . . A serious first term retention problem exists . . . in a majority of the career fields."[29] This will continue to be the case as long as military pay rates fail to be meaningfully tied to pay rates in the rest of the economy—for as long, that is, as the military payroll continues to be distributed with little relevance to the distribution of alternative employment and pay opportunities facing members of the enlisted work force.

CIVILIAN PAY SYSTEMS are not, of course, ideal, nor can they be transplanted to the defense establishment. To the contrary, the civilian econ-

27. U.S. Department of Defense, Office of Assistant Secretary of Defense for Manpower, Reserve Affairs, and Logistics, *Manpower Requirements Report for FY 1981* (DOD, 1980), p. x-4.

28. Critics of the conscription system have argued that the true economic cost imposed on the draftees is substantial and inequitably borne in the form of implicit tax. The magnitude of the cost has been described as "the difference between the earnings the draftee or draft-motivated (reluctant) volunteer receives from the military (including income in kind) and the earnings that would just cause that individual to be willing to enter the military." See Larry A. Sjaastad and Ronald W. Hansen, "The Conscription Tax: An Empirical Analysis," in *Studies Prepared for the President's Commission on an All-Volunteer Armed Force*, vol. 2 (GPO, 1970), p. iv-1-2.

29. Department of Defense, *Modernizing Military Pay*, vol. 2: *Appendices I through IX*, pp. 12–15.

omy in general is characterized by rigidities—social, institutional, political, administrative—that often impede the smooth functioning of labor markets. Moreover, by some accounts, some groups in the civilian work force of the Defense Department and in federal agencies in general may already have gained an advantageous earnings position that is not necessarily related to market conditions or dictated by important social considerations.[30] In a different vein, it may be unrealistic to assume that workers gauge alternative employment opportunities on the basis of a single occupation. Yet, however valid these considerations may be, it is the structure of earnings in the civilian sector that, for better or for worse, shapes and reflects the relative availability and market value of labor services. Alternative employment opportunities are typically gauged on the basis of existing skills and qualifications; a technician is not likely to consider a clerical job, nor is a service worker qualified for craft work. This is the status quo; the military is now an integral part of it, and the shape of the pay structure in the armed forces must accommodate to it.

30. Rather, it has been argued, many defense civilians, for example, "are being compensated at unjustifiably high levels," in part because of grade creep and "quirks in the formula now used to calculate pay increases for federal blue-collar workers." See Martin Binkin with Herschel Kanter and Rolf H. Clark, *Shaping the Defense Civilian Work Force: Economics, Politics, and National Security* (Brookings Institution, 1978), p. 72.

CHAPTER FOUR

PAYING THE MODERN MILITARY

THE PROBLEMS associated with the military compensation system beg for redress. Reform of the system of pay for enlisted personnel, essential for reasons of efficiency, is bound to improve the caliber of the force, thereby enhancing its effectiveness. Pay policy should be designed to bring military compensation in line with the nature of the occupation, the job setting, the cost of investment in manpower training, alternative employment opportunities outside the military, and the growth potential inherent in each occupation. By these criteria, different occupations would call for different pay schemes. The merits of such an arrangement for the military have been considered in the past. An arrangement consistent with prevailing practice throughout this economy is of growing relevance to the modern defense establishment.

The Value of Bonuses

Proposals for introducing occupational pay differentials in the military compensation system have been made at various times during the past quarter-century; invariably they have called for the use of special payments *outside of* rather than *integrated with* the basic pay tables. Reenlistment and enlistment bonuses, still the clearest example of the principle of special payments, are awarded on an ad hoc basis and in addition to basic pay. In part, managerial preference for offering special pay in this form has been justified on efficiency grounds; by treating and administering these pays separately from all other elements of regular military compensation, managers can modify the structure of "extraneous" financial incentives as the need arises. But perhaps the more fundamental rationale for this special arrangement lies in the notion that the military system of values is inconsistent with anything other than a *single* pay schedule: other pays and financial incentives should not distort that schedule.

Implementation of these concepts has not been without difficulties, however. The Military Compensation Policy Board in 1967 clearly articulated the dilemma of satisfying two objectives: "Arguments for special pays based on occupational qualifications within the military run counter to [the] predilection for unity. . . . Preference for uniformity of pay within a profession does not deny that an alternative employment market exists in the civilian economy. . . . Rather, a preference for uniformity denies the relevance *inside the profession* of those market results. Nonetheless, a failure to reflect market alternatives in the military pay system can result in a failure to man the system to meet its occupational requirements."[1] The board recommended the continued extension of special pays to military personnel, thus supporting the sense of professionalism that de-emphasizes occupational differences and occupational pays. But recognizing the need to satisfy manning requirements, it noted that at some future time and "if current trends continue it may be that . . . separate salary tables for various military occupational subgroups will be appropriate."[2]

Has that time arrived? Have military manning problems become severe enough to warrant incorporation of explicit pay differentials in the basic pay tables? The nature and magnitude of manning problems the armed forces face can no longer be dismissed as either temporary or inconsequential for military effectiveness. But would expanded use of differential pay provide the most effective solution to the problems?

President Carter's Commission on Military Compensation thought so. In its 1978 report the commission paid considerable attention to the impact of special pay on personnel retention. It recommended more extensive use of occupational pay differentials, noting that the basic pay line should be sufficient to attract and retain "the correct number and quality of personnel in the occupations that are easiest to fill."[3] Occupational pay distinctions should be built "on top of this single payline . . . to fill the

1. U.S. Department of Defense, *Modernizing Military Pay,* vol. 1: *Active Duty Compensation,* Report of the First Quadrennial Review of Military Compensation (DOD, 1967), p. 102.

2. Ibid., p. 103.

3. *Report of the President's Commission on Military Compensation* (Government Printing Office, 1978), p. 124.

remaining occupations."[4] The practice of across-the-board, proportionately equal pay raises would have to be abandoned if compensation policy were to be made more responsive to and consistent with manning conditions. Also the secretary of defense would have to exercise more discretion and be afforded greater flexibility in distributing "the pay raise amount within the cash element of RMC [regular military compensation] by pay grade, by occupation, by service or by other appropriate class of personnel based upon the relative manning posture of each class. . . . Such a differential allocation is important because it will allow the underpayment of some grades and occupations, as evidenced by . . . shortages, to be corrected by applying the larger raises to the more serious problems."[5] This process would "allow . . . the development of separate pay tables by service or by occupation and would allow allocation of pay raise funds differently in RMC among basic pay and the two [quarters and subsistence] allowances."[6]

Such a policy change would certainly be in the right direction. Its most obvious shortcomings—especially when large numbers of potential recipients are involved—are the requirements of periodic determination and continuous administration of differential pays. Bonuses and other special pays (which amount to only about 3 percent of the cost of military compensation) are distributed by the separate services, and their administration is not integrated with other facets of personnel management and compensation. Administrative difficulties are not so serious, however, as those of an institutional nature: bonus payments would, in effect, accentuate occupational distinctions, thus further undermining professional unity—the very problem that proponents of *limited* pay distinctions have always recognized and sought to anticipate if not altogether avoid.

Expanded use of bonuses is certain to raise the basic issue of whether the military institution is willing to concede that one skill deserves higher compensation than another at the same rank and grade levels and, more broadly, whether the reform of military pay policy should be reduced to provision of unequal pay for the same grade. This, of course, assumes that grade attainment can indeed be independent of the occupation—that all occupations are defined at all grade levels and that all servicemen can rise through the ranks to the top. But it is precisely this assumption, which is

4. Ibid., p. 124.
5. Ibid., p. 127.
6. Ibid.

Table 4-1. Distribution of White-Collar Civilian Positions in the Department of Defense, by Occupational Category and Grade Level, 1977

Occupational category	Total number of positions	Percent in general schedule grade levels			
		1–3	*4–6*	*7–9*	*10 and above*
Technical	58,478	7	40	35	18
Clerical	286,160	17	56	26	1
Craft	6,081	1	9	83	7
Other	13,468	23	54	18	5
Service and supply	7,640	33	33	28	6
General military skills	5,828	11	80	6	3

Source: Based on data provided by U.S. Department of Defense, Office of Assistant Secretary of Defense for Manpower, Reserve Affairs, and Logistics, 1978. Positions shown are staffed by full-time workers.

built into the Presidential Commission's approach, that may be its major shortcoming.

Clearly the range between starting and top positions in various occupations can be very different depending on the nature of each occupation. Direct analogies in the federal civil service employment, for instance, abound. Data on full-time white-collar employment by occupation and general schedule grade (or its equivalent) reveal significant variations among jobs in terms of lowest and highest grades of positions. Some occupations are not even defined at the lowest grades; the entry level for "electronic technicians," "interpreters," and "medical technologists," for instance, is GS-5. By contrast, over a fourth of the workers in general clerical and administrative positions are at the GS-3 level. At the other extreme, attainment of or promotion to grades above the GS-10 level is not possible in many clerical positions and other occupations in which such grades are simply not defined.[7]

The jobs held by civilians in the Department of Defense and described on the basis of the occupational classification system used for the enlisted force follow essentially the same grade pattern as those in other government agencies. They are split almost evenly between general schedule (white-collar) and wage board (blue-collar), yet a single major occupational category may include jobs graded under both systems. White-collar jobs can be found in all occupational categories; included are all clerical positions and 40 percent of the technical jobs. The differences in the distribution of grades are significant. As table 4-1 shows, close to one-fifth of

7. See U.S. Civil Service Commission, Bureau of Personnel Management Information Systems, *Occupations of Federal White-Collar Workers,* Federal Civilian Workforce Statistics, SM 56-12 (GPO, 1976), table D-1.

Table 4-2. Distribution of Blue-Collar Civilian Positions in the Department of Defense, by Occupational Category and Grade Level, 1977

		Percent in wage grade levels				
Occupational category	*Total number of positions*	*1–3*	*4–6*	*7–9*	*10–12*	*13 and above*
Technical	20,587	...	5	12	75	7
Clerical	...	...	...	...	...	...
Craft	167,899	1	7	32	58	2
Other	86,806	19	54	23	3	...
Service and supply	85,052	20	54	23	3	...
General military skills, including combat	1,754	5	57	25	12	...

Source: Based on data provided by Office of Assistant Secretary of Defense for Manpower, Reserve Affairs, and Logistics, 1978. Positions shown are staffed by full-time workers.

the technical positions are graded at the GS-10 level and above, compared to only 6 percent in the service and supply area, while practically no clerical positions are graded at or above the GS-10 level. About two-thirds of the civilian jobs in the service and supply area are concentrated below grade GS-7, but 80 percent of craft occupations are graded above the GS-8 level.

The same is true of blue-collar civilian jobs, as shown in table 4-2. The contrast between technical and craft positions, on the one hand, and general military and service and supply positions, on the other, is striking. For example, over 80 percent of technical positions and 60 percent of craft positions are graded at or above the WG-10 level, compared to only 3 percent of positions in the service and supply occupations and 12 percent in the general military skills category. In fact, over 70 percent of positions in the latter two areas combined fall between the WG-1 and WG-6 grade levels; but there are virtually no positions graded below the WG-4 level in the technical and craft areas.

Though these data may not reflect the optimal grade distribution to which enlisted jobs should eventually be made to conform, they bring into question the validity of the assumption that all military jobs should be defined at all grade levels—that, in effect, all servicemen can rise through the ranks to the top, and that it should in fact be possible for all to attain any grade level without changing occupations.

A detailed analysis of several military job categories by the widely used Hay approach reveals wide variations in job content among *different positions* at the *same grade level*. As can be seen in table 4-3, the points

Table 4-3. Hay Point Evaluation of Selected Enlisted Positions at Different Grade Levels

	Hay points at grade level[a]		
Job	E-3	E-5	E-7
Food service specialist	102	219	275
Military police	141	228	275
Infantryman (light weapons)	141	228	291
Aircraft maintenance specialist	152	230	298

Source: Hay Associates, "An Analysis of Selected Linkages between Military and Civil Service Occupations," in U.S. Department of Defense, Office of Secretary of Defense, *The Third Quadrennial Review of Military Compensation: Staff Studies and Selected Supporting Papers*, vol. 8: *Work Level Comparisons* (DOD, 1976), pp. 120–22.

a. The higher the number of points, the more demanding the job.

accumulated for expertise and problem-solving skills as well as accountability range from 102 to 152 at the E-3 level, and from 275 to 298 at the E-7 level, for food service specialist and aircraft maintenance specialist jobs, respectively.[8] The food service specialist position, according to Hay, "was evaluated as very low in total Hay Points, compared to other jobs in each grade. The job was evaluated at the extreme low end of the E-3 job sample. Further, the job had a small percentage of Accountability, being predominantly a job involving a relatively low level of Know-How."[9] On the other hand, the aircraft maintenance specialist position "was evaluated at or above the median HP value for each grade. The profile analysis revealed prominent Accountability demands at both the E-5 and E-7 levels. High problem solving demands are also noted at the E-7 level."[10]

Moreover, by Hay standards some job grades at each level appear inappropriate. These jobs are identified as outliers and include armorer-unit supply specialist and food service specialist, both of which fell significantly below the median point score of a sample of E-3 jobs, and medical service technician and air traffic control technician, both of which scored significantly above the median score assigned to E-5 jobs. According to the Hay study, the "identification of outliers may have implications for job classification in the military service. An outlier may well represent

8. The Hay method of job evaluation is based on "desk audits" and has been used worldwide by some four thousand organizations. Experience and reference data that back up the Hay analyses make them quite credible.

9. See Hay Associates, "An Analysis of Selected Linkages between Military and Civil Service Occupations," in U.S. Department of Defense, Office of Secretary of Defense, *The Third Quadrennial Review of Military Compensation: Staff Studies and Selected Supporting Papers*, vol. 8: *Work Level Comparisons* (DOD, 1976), pp. 120–21.

10. Ibid., p. 122.

Table 4-4. Rank Designation by Pay Grade in the Armed Forces

Pay grade	Army — Noncommissioned officers	Specialists	Navy[a]	Marine Corps	Air Force
E-9	Command sergeant major Sergeant major	...	Master chief petty officer	Sergeant major Master gunnery sergeant	Chief master sergeant
E-8	First sergeant Master sergeant	...	Senior chief petty officer	First sergeant Master sergeant	Senior master sergeant
E-7	Platoon sergeant Sergeant first class	Specialist 7	Chief petty officer	Gunnery sergeant	Master sergeant
E-6	Staff sergeant	Specialist 6	Petty officer, first class	Staff sergeant	Technical sergeant
E-5	Sergeant	Specialist 5	Petty officer, second class	Sergeant	Staff sergeant
E-4	Corporal	Specialist 4	Petty officer, third class	Corporal	Sergeant
E-3	Private first class		Seaman[b]	Lance corporal	Airman first class
E-2	Private, PV-2		Seaman apprentice[b]	Private first class	Airman
E-1	Private, PV-1		Seaman recruit[b]	Private	Airman basic

Sources: U.S. Department of Defense, Washington Headquarters Services, Directorate for Information, Operations and Reports, *Selected Manpower Statistics FY 1979* (DOD, 1980), p. 86.

a. Titles for petty officers denote "rating" (naval skill) such as boatswain, gunner's mate, yeoman, storekeeper, etc. Personnel in seaman categories are not considered as possessing ratings.

b. Also includes airman, construction man, dental man, fireman, hospital man, and stewardsman and apprentices and recruits in these categories.

a misclassification. . . . Such jobs should be reviewed to determine if re-classification is desirable."[11]

Misclassification of jobs is certainly not a problem unique to the armed forces. Yet, job misclassification may be more of a symptom in the armed forces than anywhere else. If this is so, reform of the system of military compensation should be focused on the grade structure of enlisted occupations. Before the issue of differential pay can be settled, the traditional, albeit now questionable, bond among rank, pay grade, occupation, and military compensation must be loosened.

Rank and Pay Grade

On the surface, the nature of the link between rank and pay grade appears simple enough. In the military jargon, rank "means the order of precedence among members of the uniformed services," while "grade means a step or degree in a graduated scale of office or rank, that is established as grade by law or regulation."[12] Or, in even simpler terms, rank is a title (for example, staff sergeant) while grade designates the pay line. In practice, rank and grade are related on a one-to-one basis; they are thus considered one and the same. Each of the nine enlisted-level grades (E-1 through E-9) has a rank designation, as shown in table 4-4.

In theory, this correspondence rests on the assumption that on attainment of a given rank an enlisted person has acquired a particular and necessary set of qualifications (mastery over tasks, specialized knowledge, expertise, or more generally a skill level); thusly qualified the worker is worthy of a higher title (rank) and greater compensation (at the higher pay grade). "There is universal agreement," the Military Compensation Policy Board noted in 1967, "that work level (military pay grade) is one proper basis for salary discrimination. Plant managers earn more than foremen because their work is expected to contribute more to attainment of the company's objectives than is the work of foremen. Generals get paid more than second lieutenants because generals are expected to con-

11. Ibid., p. 123.

12. *Pay and Allowances of the Uniformed Services Pursuant to Title 37, United States Code (Public Law 87-649 (76 Stat. 451)) as Amended Through June 30, 1977 and Supplementary Material,* prepared for the House Committee on Armed Services (GPO, 1977), p. 3.

tribute more to the accomplishment of the military's mission than are second lieutenants."[13]

That positions in the armed forces are graded and that those who staff such positions are accorded titles is not particularly noteworthy; similar practices are followed in most large organizations. Indeed, military grades serve a purpose analogous to that of civil service ratings in federal employment. Though the concept may be one and the same, there are important differences in the manner in which it is implemented in the military and elsewhere.

Grades in civilian organizations are, certainly in principle and usually in practice as well, determined primarily on the basis of job-related factors. These principles governing classification of positions in the federal government were set forth in 1920: positions and not individuals should be classified; the duties and responsibilities pertaining to a position constitute the outstanding characteristics that distinguish it from, or mark its similarity to, other positions; the qualifications for a position are an important factor in the determination of the classification of the position; and the individual characteristics of an employee occupying a position should have no bearing on the classification of the position.[14] It follows that among civilian jobs the grade structure will differ to the extent jobs differ from one another. In the armed forces, with their emphasis on the institutional rather than the occupational nature of military service, the focus is not on jobs but, rather, on the service members themselves. Accordingly, the military personnel management system emphasizes horizontal equality and vertical hierarchy. To maintain horizontal equality, occupational differences are played down and "equal pay for equal grade" is guaranteed. As for maintaining hierarchy, an explicit system of ranks—a system that defines the exact order of precedence—is in place across all services throughout the military institution and, what is especially significant, across all occupations within each service. In such a system the focus is, by necessity, not on jobs but on individuals.

Inevitably, then, hierarchical order becomes, in and by itself, a major goal but at the same time an overwhelmingly constraining factor in the military personnel management system. The system functions so as to

13. *Active Duty Compensation*, p. 101.

14. See *Report of the Congressional Joint Commission on Reclassification of Salaries, Submitting a Classification of Positions on the Basis of Duties and Qualifications, and Schedules of Compensation for the Respective Classes*, H. Doc. 686, 66 Cong. 2 sess. (GPO, 1920), pt. 1, p. 72.

ensure that each member's potential in terms of advancement through the ranks over the course of a military career is equally promising: today's private, whether technician, craftsman, or clerk, can become tomorrow's sergeant major. The logic appears to be even more compelling since enlisted individuals often serve in jobs outside of their primary occupation, and they carry their rank title with them. It is then only natural that parallel promotion time paths be an integral part of the personnel management system.

Parallel paths of promotion in a system that links rank and pay grade mean parallel pay opportunities. This is precisely what is reflected in the occupational earnings distributions in tables 3-2 and 3-3; jobs are virtually indistinguishable from one another because they are the product of an inherently equal distribution of titles and, more broadly, of a hierarchical order defined not on the basis of individual occupations but on the basis of collective institutional affiliation and longevity in the service. As can be seen in table 4-5, in all of the occupational categories the heaviest concentration of personnel is at the rank of corporal; most of the variation occurs below that rank, largely because of the high turnover rates among first-term enlisted personnel. At the other end of the spectrum, the proportion of personnel with the rank of sergeant major is remarkably constant across all occupations with the exception of the clerical category. And as table 4-6 shows, the mean pay grade also varies little by occupation, from 4.0 for general military skills to 4.8 for clerical personnel and electronics equipment repairmen alike.

The strong link between rank and pay grade that is manifested in tables 4-5 and 4-6 has unduly constrained the military compensation system for quite some time. Pay grades E-8 and E-9 were introduced in the Military Pay Act of 1959, and corresponding rank titles for armed forces personnel began to appear as the new pay grades were filled. In 1957 the U.S. Defense Advisory Committee on Professional and Technical Compensation had identified a "dual problem of lowered prestige and insufficient monetary award" for many servicemen who were "reaching the top rung of their ladder at a young age with little opportunity for further advancement. . . . The existing top grade lacks a monetary reward of a significance such as to cause it to be appealing to the young man starting up the ladder."[15] It recommended the addition of the E-8 and E-9 grades and

15. *Report of the Defense Advisory Committee on Professional and Technical Compensation,* vol. 1: *Military Personnel* (GPO, 1957), p. 65.

Table 4-5. Distribution of Enlisted Personnel in the Armed Forces, by Rank Title and Occupational Category, 1978

Percent

Occupational category	Private PV-1	Private PV-2	Private first class	Corporal	Sergeant	Staff sergeant	Sergeant first class	Master sergeant	Sergeant major
					Rank title[a]				
General military specialists, including combat	5	10	22	29	16	9	6	2	1
Electronics equipment repairmen	1	3	15	26	25	17	9	3	1
Communications and intelligence specialists	3	7	20	26	21	13	7	2	1
Medical and dental specialists	3	6	20	28	22	12	7	2	1
Other technical and allied specialists	2	6	18	24	23	16	9	2	1
Administrative specialists and clerks	2	5	15	23	22	16	11	3	2
Electrical and mechanical repairmen	3	8	22	25	21	12	6	2	1
Craftsmen	3	8	20	24	21	14	7	2	1
Service and supply handlers	2	8	22	28	20	11	6	1	1

Source: Based on data provided by Office of Assistant Secretary of Defense for Manpower, Reserve Affairs, and Logistics, 1979.

a. Army rank titles are shown here; titles vary by service.

Table 4-6. Average Pay Grade of Enlisted Personnel, by Occupational Category, 1978

Occupational category	Average pay grade
Technical	
Electronic equipment repairmen	4.8
Communications and intelligence specialists	4.4
Medical and dental specialists	4.3
Other technical and allied specialists	4.6
Clerical	
Administrative specialists and clerks	4.8
Craft	
Electrical and mechanical repairmen	4.3
Other	4.4
Other	
General military specialists, including combat[a]	4.0
Service and supply handlers	4.2

Source: Based on data provided by Office of Assistant Secretary of Defense for Manpower, Reserve Affairs, and Logistics, 1979.

a. Officially entitled "infantry, gun crews, and seamanship specialists."

the corresponding adjustments in the pay scale as central features of a program that would "pay people what their services are actually worth, instead of paying people on the basis of longevity of service, and in this way encourage and reward outstanding performance, advanced skills, and military careers for high quality personnel."[16]

The committee did not, of course, advocate the indiscriminate addition of E-8 and E-9 positions across the board, and in all occupational categories. Nor did military leaders so interpret the recommendations or the law in which they were embodied. The Army's senior personnel official pointed out in 1959 that Army "positions which warrant these [additional] E-8 and E-9 grades are being carefully and systematically identified through comprehensive job evaluation and review of unit organizational tables."[17] And a Marine Corps representative noted: "These new pay grades are very important to us . . . we were able to relieve the compression . . . [and] to establish these two ranks as command assistants and as technical assistants. . . . We are insuring that the billets we create in these two ranks are very bona fide military requirements. We have just determined how many of these E-8s and E-9s we will have in the technical

16. Ibid., p. vii.

17. Testimony by Lieutenant General James F. Collins, U.S. Army, *Department of Defense Appropriations for 1960*, pt. 3: *Manpower, Personnel and Reserves, Hearings* before the Subcommittee on Department of Defense Appropriations of the Senate Committee on Appropriations, 86 Cong. 1 sess. (GPO, 1960), p. 93.

area. We have used a very thorough screening process."[18] A senior Air Force official presented a scheme for the allocation of the new grades:

This authorization relieves the compression . . . and it allows better career progression for selected senior noncommissioned officers. . . . To realize the maximum benefit of this new authorization, . . . these new pay grades have been allocated as follows:[19]

	Grades (percent)	
Area	E-8	E-9
Highly technical	65	73
Technical	23	20
Semitechnical	12	7
Total	100	100

While far from disclosing blueprints for managerial action, these military leaders clearly articulated the prevailing sentiment that differentiation in career and compensation opportunities consistent with skill development and skill attainment was needed. And even though the most explicit plan, that of the Air Force, was only broadly framed around occupational areas, the implication was clear: the more technical the jobs, the higher the content of E-8 and E-9 positions would be.

That the new career and pay opportunities would eventually be aligned with rank titles was explicit in Army and Marine Corps policy. Each service delineated two career paths, one producing technical, the other nontechnical senior enlisted servicemen; the insignia would be visibly different and rank titles would vary but pay would not. The Army's representative exhibited a chart of the new rank titles, pay grades, and insignia, explaining that "the selection to these grades will be limited to those . . . who will act as leaders and supervisors in broad areas of *command* or *technical skills*. We will have four ranks in these grades, first sergeant and sergeant major, the senior command assistants, and the master sergeant and master gunnery sergeant who will be the senior technical assistants."[20] The rules that had always governed attainment of, and progression through, the ranks inevitably would govern selection for the top two ranks.

Yet, as necessary and important as the attainment and recognition of

18. Testimony by Major General Donald M. Weller, U.S. Marine Corps, ibid., p. 446.

19. Testimony by Major General Joseph J. Nazarro, U.S. Air Force, ibid., pp. 495–96. Emphasis added.

20. Ibid., pp. 438–39. Emphasis added.

Table 4-7. Distribution of Enlisted Personnel in Pay Grades E-8 and E-9, by Occupational Category, 1978

Percent

Occupational category	Pay grade	
	E-8	*E-9*
Technical	28	27
Electronics equipment repairmen	12	13
Communications and intelligence specialists	9	8
Medical and dental specialists	4	3
Other technical and allied specialists	3	3
Clerical	26	36
Administrative specialists and clerks	26	36
Craft	22	22
Electrical and mechanical repairmen	18	18
Other craftsmen	4	4
Other	23	15
General military specialists, including combat[a]	16	10
Service and supply handlers	7	5

Source· Based on data provided by Office of Assistant Secretary of Defense for Manpower, Reserve Affairs, and Logistics, 1979.

a. Officially entitled "infantry, gun crews, and seamanship specialists."

individual rank titles may be, the practice of linking rank with the grade classification of military positions can no longer be reconciled with manning objectives. Before World War II the concept of military manpower implied a high degree of occupational homogeneity. The prerequisites for rank attainment in a system stressing general military duties and ground combat operations could well coincide with the prerequisites for skill development. But the occupational diversification and specialization that now characterize the armed forces call into serious question the pattern of allocation of enlisted grades and of the top grades in particular. As table 4-7 shows, over a quarter of all the E-8 positions and 36 percent of the E-9 positions are now allocated to the clerical occupational area. On the other hand, craft jobs are allocated slightly more than a fifth of the E-8 or the E-9 positions. Moreover, even when *highly technical* is defined as encompassing all of the technical occupational areas, only 28 percent of the E-8 positions and 27 percent of the E-9 positions fall within highly technical categories. And within each occupational area (with the exception of clerical positions) the number of E-8 and E-9 positions appears to be almost fixed at between 2 percent and 4 percent of the total. The reason for this is the simple fact that in the armed forces, grades—like titles—are used to classify individuals rather than jobs.

Neither the rank nor pay grade distributions can be construed as deriving from the nature of modern enlisted job requirements. This places a heavy burden on military personnel managers; their programs—even their long-range plans—are necessarily focused on people instead of on jobs. This is particularly the case in the Air Force where grade structure policy is explicitly formulated in terms of workers: "On a long-range basis, the aggregate *number of grades for personnel on active duty* . . . *will be determined by the promotion system,* i.e., sufficient grades will be provided so as to insure stated promotion opportunity."[21] The obvious reason for that and similar policies is the need to sustain the hierarchical structure of the military institution. No matter how important that is, it is imperative that the military realign its pay grade structure. To achieve both objectives, the bond between rank and pay grade should be loosened.

Skill and Pay Grade

The link between rank and pay grade is not intrinsic to the military compensation system. The system provides for equal pay at each grade level; it does not bind military managers to assign rank titles that match pay grades, or vice versa. This link is a by-product of military personnel management policies that ensure that an individual in any occupation can rise through the ranks. But even under current policies that allow any private to become a first sergeant, there is no requirement that the private be an E-1 and the first sergeant an E-9. Clearly the grade of an enlisted jobholder should depend on the job he fills, not on the rank he attains.

To change the manpower management system would not be demanding, from either an administrative or an institutional standpoint. Not only is the current system almost completely amenable to change, it invites it. Breaking the bond between rank and pay grade should involve nothing more than realigning the grade structure of enlisted jobs; it need not hinge on modifying the pay tables. In addition, realignment of job grades can be implemented without disturbing the rank distribution and titles of enlisted personnel. Not only will the change improve efficiency but it will

---

21. U.S. Department of the Air Force, *The USAF Personnel Plan,* vol. 1: *Personnel Management Objectives* (Department of the Air Force, n.d.), pp. 3–7. Emphasis added.

also contribute to the preservation of what is perhaps the most highly valued institutional feature in the armed forces—the rank system.

As a first step, it is necessary that military managers explicitly treat rank titles and grade ratings as distinct and separate from one another. Rank attainment has always depended on longevity in the armed forces; indeed, within each service, tenure constitutes a near-perfect explanatory variable of an individual's rank. This should continue to be the case, thereby preserving the means by which enlisted personnel assert their institutional affiliation. On the other hand, grade ratings should be made to depend strictly on personal qualifications and performance, thereby improving the pay system's ability to match enlisted workers and jobs. Service in the armed forces would thus imply equal opportunity for promotion through the ranks but differential opportunity for grade attainment; today's private could still become tomorrow's first sergeant, but grade would vary without regard for rank.

There are some indications that the system and the people who manage it are ready for such a reform. In some ways, attempts to reconcile personnel qualifications and performance with grade assignment are already evident. In part, the growing participation of women in the armed forces may have forced the issue. A Department of Defense assessment of policies regarding the use of women by the armed forces noted that "a higher percentage of women *enter at an advanced pay grade* for education and experience. . . . The average female recruit is about a year older than her male counterpart . . . much more likely to have graduated from high school and scored about ten points higher on the entrance tests."[22] In 1976, enlisted women in the Army tended to have a higher pay level than enlisted men with the same number of years of service. The mean pay grade of men with one year of service was 1.80 and that of women 2.03; with two years of service, 3.15 and 3.43; three years, 3.81 and 3.99; four years, 4.24 and 4.50; five years, 4.59 and 4.84; and six years, 4.88 and 5.02.[23]

These differences in the mean pay grades of men and women are revealing inasmuch as they indicate that grade attainment can vary on the basis of personnel qualifications and performance. While the higher pay grades of enlisted women still mean they have higher ranks than their male coun-

22. U.S. Department of Defense, Office of Assistant Secretary of Defense for Manpower, Reserve Affairs, and Logistics, *Use of Women in the Military,* 2d ed. (DOD, 1978), pp. 7, 22. Emphasis added.
23. Ibid., p. 7.

terparts, it would not be difficult to reconcile different distributions by rank and pay grade.

Indeed, it would not be difficult to reconcile any pay grade distribution with the existing rank distribution. For example, if pay grades were based only on job characteristics, it would be possible to distribute mean pay grade by occupation in such a way that, at the rank of corporal, the average pay grade for technical jobs would be E-6; for clerical jobs, E-3; for craft jobs, E-5; for service and supply jobs, E-3; and for general military skills, including combat, E-4. Any other combination of average pay grades might as easily apply at that rank; the point is that pay grades would be assigned regardless of rank. By the same analogy, two individuals could be paid at the same grade level but be awarded different rank titles.

Realignment of job grades is an undertaking that can only be carried out by the military services. Each service's judgments about its own optimal structure of job grades would have to be based on thorough and detailed assessment of its mission demands and position requirements, and independently of inventory. There are a number of guidelines that the services should observe as they work out their blueprints for change.

They should set out to make the distribution of grades more rational. Neither the number of positions nor the number of grades need change. But the proportion of top grades should be greatest in those occupations where the cost of training workers is highest and where, consequently, long careers are most appropriate. To this end, an increase in the number of top grades (possibly at the E-7 level and above) would be warranted in those occupations where current retention problems can be identified; not by accident, the most serious of them arise in those areas where manpower training costs are highest.[24] Similarly, in occupations where exceptionally stringent physical requirements or where low training costs render short-term careers more appropriate, there should be a relatively high concentration of lower grades—everything else being equal—corresponding to positions that would be staffed by relatively younger individuals.

24. The loss rate among enlisted personnel in the craft occupational category is approximately 21 percent compared to 19 percent in the clerical area and 20 percent for technical workers (based on data provided by Office of Assistant Secretary of Defense for Manpower, Reserve Affairs, and Logistics, 1978. Yet the cost of training clerical personnel is lower and the probability that any jobs in that category can or should be graded at the E-7 level and above is smaller.

To alter the balance of positions, a number of job slots in the top three grades now allocated to the clerical area could be transferred to the technical and craft areas. Individuals who perform clerical work would continue to be eligible for promotion to the top rank, but the total cost of sustaining clerical positions would go down. The obvious question of course is how many workers would continue to choose to follow a lengthy career in the clerical area. Yet the fundamental question is whether, everything else being equal, long careers are warranted in that area (in relation to other occupational areas) and ought to be encouraged through grade advancement. Grade restructuring of military jobs is likely to reveal the possibilities as well as the need for occupational mobility in the services. While a worker in electronics could advance, say, to the E-9 grade level during the course of his career, a person in service and supply might reach only the E-5 grade level. For the latter worker, further advancement in grade (as opposed to promotion through the ranks) would require occupational mobility. This is a regular route to advancement in civilian employment that should be more readily available to the military (for qualified workers and subject to the availability of positions) through the variety of training curricula offered.

Severing the link between rank and pay grade in the armed forces need not affect the future distribution of rank titles. At worst, the constraints governing rank attainment would remain unchanged. It is possible, however, that if title awards are made independently of budgetary considerations, merit would play a more significant role than it now does. Thus to the extent that promotion through the ranks would depend on merit and longevity exclusively, promotion opportunities could in fact widen. Indeed, the entire rank structure could be reviewed and the appropriate, unconstrained objectives of the rank system could be reaffirmed or, if warranted, reformulated.

With ranks marking an individual's path throughout a military career, grades would be the logical indicators of achievement in an occupational area. When careers are spanned by more than one occupation, as is often the case in the armed forces, and when attainment of the top grades requires proficiency in a wide variety of jobs and supervisory responsibilities, a separate pay grade track offers managerial flexibility. Attainment of a particular rank need not coincide with attainment of some designated level of proficiency. To the extent that the two important tools—promotion policy and pay grade policy—could be used separately, personnel management could become more effective.

Breaking the bond between rank and pay grade would promote efficiency in the allocation of human resources in the armed services. Perceptions of the nature of the manpower available to the armed forces and of the jobs to be filled would govern manpower policy. The relationship between age and productivity suggests that the armed forces would gain in terms of military effectiveness if they used their workers for longer periods of time. The vast majority of military jobs require expertise that only careerists can possess. By allowing occupational requirements, rather than rank titles, to determine the composition and compensation of the enlisted force, the armed services can improve the quality of their personnel.

The benefits likely to accrue from expanded opportunities in areas where the need for experienced personnel is pressing could be significant. A higher proportion of top grades would substantially increase the financial incentives needed to improve retention. The corresponding reductions in the proportion of lower grades would reduce the number of new recruits needed annually.

The role of bonuses as financial incentives could be preserved, although their use could be concentrated in very specific areas that call for a short-term commitment of a very special nature. Enlistments and reenlistments in the area of combat arms, for example, could be encouraged through the use of bonuses, in harmony with the notion that soldiers should be a youthful and vigorous force even in today's armies.

NONE of these changes can be accomplished overnight, but neither is it necessary that they be. The transition can be as gradual as the pattern of personnel losses due to retirement dictates. Since the grades of those now serving in the military should not be changed, positions should be subject to grade reclassification only as incumbents retire. Though the changes would not affect opportunities for promotion in rank, they could materially affect prospects for advancement in grade. Upgrading one position in a system with a fixed distribution of grades would require that another position be downgraded. This would enhance prospects for grade advancement in the one instance but limit them in the other.

In the long run it might be necessary to relax the assumption of a fixed relation between budget and pay grades. To the extent that the military manpower budget is allowed to increase in real terms, and assuming that a reasonable pattern of changes in pay grade would be inconsistent with across-the-board, equal pay increases, it might be possible to allocate increases exactly as the President's Commission on Military Compensation recommended, by applying larger increases to the more serious problems.[25]

As retention improved and reached permanently higher levels, the number of unproductive personnel in the pipeline would be reduced. Either additional positions could be created to absorb individuals with rank titles and grades who had not been serving in jobs, or there could be a permanent reduction in total strength. If the possibilities for improving retention via changes in the military grade structure and the pay system and thus improving the caliber of the enlisted force by enriching its level of experience appear promising, the military retirement system should also be revised. The practice of controlling retention and encouraging youthfulness that has for so long been legitimized and epitomized in the military retirement system has become counterproductive. Restructuring the military pay system to support the occupational goals of the armed forces demands a corollary overhauling of the military retirement system.

25. *Report of the President's Commission on Military Compensation,* p. 127.

CHAPTER FIVE

MODERNIZING MILITARY RETIREMENT

REALIGNMENT of the grade structure of military occupations should go beyond reframing the pay policy. Indeed, a new grade structure aimed at higher retention and longer tenure could serve as the cornerstone of a general reform of the military compensation system. Military retirement policy, in particular, should be harmonized with pay policies to remove the incentives for skilled people—some at the peak of their productivity—to leave the service early.

The Retirement Plan

The U.S. armed forces provide their members with one of the nation's most generous pension plans. After just twenty years of service, a retiree is in practice immediately entitled to a lifetime annuity which is protected against inflation and to which the annuitant did not contribute explicitly. Under this virtually unique system the typical enlisted annuitant retires at forty years of age and spends more years in retirement than he spent in active service.[1] In addition, as a full participant in the social security system he is entitled to the same benefits as civilians covered by that program. The military retiree also carries into retirement such benefits as free or reduced-rate medical care, subsidized commissaries, low-cost housing loans and life insurance, and job preference.

The financial advantage of the military plan over other large retirement

1. It is often claimed that plans covering police and firefighters are at least as liberal as the military plan. Although it is difficult to generalize about such a large and diverse group of plans, the typical police-firefighter plan provides for normal retirement at age 50 or 55 after completing 20 to 25 years of service, and generally there are no early retirement provisions. Moreover, automatic cost-of-living increases are the exception rather than the rule. See Robert Tilove, *Public Employee Pension Funds* (Columbia University Press, 1976), p. 222.

Table 5-1. Lifetime Retirement Earnings of Typical Enlisted Personnel under Various Plans[a]

Dollars

	Lifetime retirement earnings			
	Undiscounted		Discounted[b]	
Plan	After 20 years	After 30 years	After 20 years	After 30 years
U.S. military	187,400	310,000	89,500	171,400
Other U.S. plans				
Typical private	11,700	42,000	2,700	15,700
Typical nonfederal public service	16,200	58,200	4,100	23,400
Federal civil service	18,300	69,000	4,200	24,900
Typical policeman or fireman[c]	69,000	224,300	24,800	128,200
Australian military	256,800	322,500	115,900	171,600
Canadian military	118,900	244,400	52,500	132,500

Source: Data provided by Congressional Budget Office, December 1979.

a. The typical enlisted retiree entered the service at age 19, progressed through the system at the median pay grade, and retired after 20 or 30 years of service. Prices are assumed to have grown 5 percent annually and wages 6 percent; costs are deflated to 1978 dollars

b. Discounted at 5 percent.

c. Based on a 1972 survey of 42 systems covering more than 250,000 policemen and firemen; Robert Tilove, *Public Employee Pension Funds* (Columbia University Press, 1976), pp. 222–40.

plans is apparent in table 5-1. The lifetime earnings of an enlisted person retiring after twenty years' service are at least an order of magnitude larger than those under most civilian plans, and the military plan also compares quite favorably with police and firefighter plans. While the differences narrow for the individual who serves for thirty years before retiring, the advantage of military retirement remains sizable. Ample military retirement pensions are not unique to the U.S. armed forces; the Australian plan, in fact, is even more liberal.

The military retirement plan has not always been so generous. Before 1935, military personnel had to serve a minimum of thirty years (and in some cases forty years) before they were entitled to retire. In 1935, to reduce the hump of officers who had entered the service during World War I, legislation was enacted authorizing the voluntary retirement of Army officers with as little as fifteen years of service. Though it was suspended during World War II, the law remained in effect until 1948.[2]

2. The legislative history of the military retirement system is a complex patchwork of laws relating to regular and reserve officers and enlisted personnel of the different services. For a brief discussion of this history, see U.S. Department of Defense, Office of Secretary of Defense, *Military Compensation Background Papers: Compensation Elements and Related Manpower Cost Items, Their Purpose and Background* (DOD, 1976), pp. 183–202.

The statute enacted in 1948 that institutionalized the modern nondisability retirement system ignored recommendations of the Advisory Commission on Service Pay (called the Hook Commission after its chairman, Charles R. Hook) that officers be permitted to retire either with thirty years of service or at the age of sixty with twenty years of service and enlisted members with either twenty-five years of service or at the age of fifty with twenty years of service.[3] While the Army went along with those recommendations, the Air Force and Navy held "that a 30-year retirement system would stifle promotions, preclude the orderly transfer of members to the reserves, and depress recruiting and retention of younger enlisted members."[4]

The perceived need for a youthful and vigorous military establishment also undoubtedly influenced Congress. With World War II and the popularized image of the combat infantryman still fresh in the minds of legislators, arguments for maintaining a youthful force were persuasive. Early retirement was considered to be a logical mechanism for controlling the vigor and physical ability of the armed forces to wage war.

Also, relatively low military pay may have helped to shape the 1948 legislation. Retirement benefits, however substantial, might not have seemed out of line in a system of compensation whose other elements, particularly those paid in cash, were considered to be inordinately low. Moreover, relatively large retirement annuities were justified to offset the perceived differences in the earning capacity of the military retiree when compared with his contemporaries in the private sector.

The record holds little to indicate that financial implications were weighed. With just 1.4 million men under arms, however, 1948 was a trough year for postwar U.S. military strength; only the clairvoyant could have predicted the bulging retirement rolls that were to develop two decades later, largely as a consequence of fielding the largest standing army in U.S. history.

Through the 1950s and the early 1960s, few challenged the retirement system itself; the principal issue with respect to military retirement during that period was how to adjust annuities. As defense manpower costs started to mount in the late 1960s, however, criticism of military retire-

3. U.S. Advisory Commission on Service Pay, *Career Compensation for the Uniformed Forces*, vol. 1: *Report and Recommendation for the Secretary of Defense* (Government Printing Office, 1948), pp. 43–45.

4. *Report of the President's Commission on Military Compensation* (GPO, 1978), p. 52.

ment became widespread as various study groups and commissions scored the system for its inefficiency and inequity.

Problems with the Status Quo

The growing concern about defense manpower costs was reflected in six major studies of the system conducted between 1967 and 1979. A high degree of attention was directed toward the military retirement system in all of them. While each group took a somewhat different view of the issues, their criticisms centered particularly on those aspects of the retirement plan that provide generous annuities to service members who serve at least twenty years but none to those who serve less. Once military personnel have served, say, ten years, few elect to leave voluntarily, fewer are discharged involuntarily, and most retire either upon or soon after reaching entitlement at twenty years.

While all but the earliest study advocated vesting at ten rather than twenty years, the proposals differed on how the vested benefits should be paid.[5] One would have provided those serving between ten and nineteen years the choice between a lump-sum payment and a deferred annuity payable at age sixty.[6] A Retirement Modernization Act proposed by the Ford administration would have established the same deferred annuity, but it would have made a cash payment available only to those separated *involuntarily* between their fifth and nineteenth years of service.[7] A proposed alternative to that bill advocated a similar plan, but it would have limited benefits for *involuntary* separatees to those who served at least ten years.[8] In a departure from this pattern, a commission appointed by President Carter proposed a deferred compensation *trust fund* that could be drawn on after ten years of service whether or not the individual sepa-

---

5. The first study, undertaken at the request of Congress, was U.S. Department of Defense, *Modernizing Military Pay,* Report of the First Quadrennial Review of Military Compensation (DOD, 1967).

6. See *Report of the President on the Study of Uniformed Services Retirement and Survivor Benefits by the Interagency Committee* (Interagency Committee, 1976). The committee was established by the Nixon administration.

7. The Retirement Modernization Act was prepared from a Department of Defense study in response to the Interagency Committee's report.

8. See Defense Manpower Commission, *Defense Manpower: The Keystone of National Security,* Report to the President and the Congress, April 1976 (GPO, 1976). The commission was established by Congress.

rated from the armed forces.[9] The administration's version of this proposal, the Uniformed Services Retirement Benefits Act of 1979, endorses the trust fund in principle, but it would permit full cash withdrawal at any time after ten years of service, in contrast to the 50 percent maximum proposed by the commission.[10]

All in all, the common thread running through the proposals is that the military retirement system needs to be changed. A consensus exists regarding the need to encourage longer careers, on the one hand, and to provide some benefits to those who serve less than twenty years, on the other. And there is widespread agreement that to achieve these ends, annuities should be reduced for younger retirees and increased for older ones, and members should be vested after completing ten years of service. To be sure, some issues are left hanging—the number of years that the individual should be required to serve to qualify for an annuity, whether early withdrawal of vested benefits should be allowed and, if so, in what form. Yet this is because of disagreement on aspects of implementation rather than on the need to change the status quo.

How is it, then, that despite all the attention devoted to the military retirement system and the repeated calls for reform, its basic features have remained virtually unchanged for three decades? Why have only two major pieces of legislation reached Capitol Hill? Why did the Retirement Modernization Act, submitted to Congress in 1973, die in the armed services committees following three years of almost complete neglect, and why does the Uniformed Services Retirement Benefits Act seem likely to meet a similar fate?

Both the 1973 proposal and its 1979 counterpart face obstacles that almost foredoom them to failure. The extreme complexity of the military retirement system makes proposals to change it difficult to understand. The constituency favoring retirement reform is neither widespread nor well organized. The military establishment opposes reform of compensation in general and of retirement in particular. While the typical taxpayer may feel that benefits are overly generous, the feelings apparently do not run deep enough to foster active citizen involvement. And any lobbying by the administration in behalf of retirement reform is likely to be low keyed since higher priority is traditionally placed on legislation related to strategy and hardware than to manpower. Nor has congressional spon-

9. *Report of the President's Commission on Military Compensation.*
10. See Uniformed Services Retirement Benefits Act.

Table 5-2. Cost of Military Compensation, by Component, Fiscal 1968 and 1978

	Fiscal 1968		Fiscal 1978	
Component	*Amount (millions of dollars)*	*Percent*	*Amount (millions of dollars)*	*Percent*
Regular military compensation	16,707	78	25,796	64
Basic pay	11,432	53	17,392	43
Allowances and tax advantage	5,275	25	8,404	21
Special pay	1,370	6	1,117	3
Retired pay	2,095	10	9,240	23
Other benefits	1,220	6	4,249	10
Total compensation	21,392	100	40,402[a]	100

Sources: U.S. Department of Defense, *Modernizing Military Pay*, vol. 1: *Active Duty Compensation*, Report of the First Quadrennial Review of Military Compensation (DOD, 1967), p. 39; table 2-1, above.
a. Differs from total shown in table 2-1 because "other allowances" category, by convention, is not considered to be compensation.

sorship of legislation been enthusiastic—no influential member of Congress took up the cause of the 1973 bill and none appears to be enthusiastically supporting the 1979 proposal.

Yet, perhaps more significant than the lack of a constituency for reform of the military retirement system may be the orientation of reform proposals toward cost savings. In a way, the emphasis on cost may be justifiable. Substantial growth in the cost of fringe benefits in general and of retirement pay in particular has resulted in a dramatic shift in the composition of the military pay package. In contrast to 1968, when over three-fourths of total payroll costs was in the form of regular military compensation and only one-sixth was spent on benefits, in 1978 fully one-third of total compensation was spent on benefits, with retirement pay accounting for close to 25 percent, while salaries amounted to only 64 percent of the total (see table 5-2).[11] These trends have aroused widespread concern about both the efficacy and the viability of the status quo. The fact that a fivefold increase in the cost of military retirement pay far outran the cost increase in any other element of military compensation—and, most notably, in active-duty pay—has been sufficiently disquieting to prompt calls for military retirement reform.

11. The growth in retirement outlays can be attributed to the doubling of retirement rolls, which grew from about 625,000 in 1968 to over 1,200,000 in 1978; cost-of-living adjustments, which exerted upward pressure on retirement pay costs, were reinforced by double-digit inflation, and were intensified by a quirk in the formula that effectively raised annuities at a rate greater than necessary to maintain constant purchasing power; and substantial increases in active-duty pay rates, on which annuities of retirees are initially based.

But excessive preoccupation with containing costs may not necessarily guarantee a successful reform package. Skeptics doubt that the savings promised would ever be achieved. In fact, because of grandfathering provisions, retirement reforms invariably give rise to near-term costs. Nor does it follow that the cheapest retirement plan is the best plan, so that reforms aimed principally at reducing costs may fail to be convincing.

Like its predecessors, the 1979 proposal emphasizes the need to contain the budgetary cost of retirement outlays and incorporates the widespread concern about equity in the distribution of retirement benefits. But neither saving money nor extending benefits to all personnel can, in and by themselves, constitute the sole legitimate goals of retirement reform. An efficient system of retirement benefits should help the services to achieve the maximum in force readiness within a given budget. The retirement system should, then, be tailored to the force composition that the pay system is designed to support. But what constitutes a desirable or appropriate force composition? Interestingly, the President's Commission found "little evidence that the distribution of ages and grades in the current structure is needed for actual work requirements." Yet it did not choose "to structure a plan for achieving a particular force profile."[12] But failure to address the larger issues relating the retirement system to the grade and age structure of the armed forces can ironically be a major contributing factor to the preservation of the status quo.

Nature of Reform

These problems can be overcome. First and foremost, reform of the retirement system should focus on national security, on helping to attract a more experienced force to a military career by a more appropriate balance of pay and benefits. The system also should be simpler, easier to understand, more equitable, and its costs more predictable. As such, it should not only be appealing to military leaders and legislators, but should gain the support of the secretary of defense.

When Should Annuities Be Paid?

Four of the six recent studies of the military retirement system have recommended the continuance of an immediate annuity after twenty years

12. "A Preliminary Report of the President's Commission on Military Compensation," March 14, 1978, pp. 18, 19.

of service, thus preserving the basic structure of the current system. Each, however, proposed a two-step plan, calling for a low annuity immediately after the end of active service to be increased at a later time. The Defense Manpower Commission and the President's Commission—the two study groups in which the Pentagon did not participate directly—recommended that eligibility for immediate annuities be tied to age and years of service, generally along the lines of the federal civilian retirement plan (the Defense Manpower Commission excluded combat personnel from this recommendation).

Early retirement, albeit at reduced annuity levels, continues to be justified largely as a means of preserving a relatively young force to meet the physical demands of military duty; as a "significant attraction and retention feature of the compensation system";[13] as compensation for the special institutional characteristics of military life; and as a financial cushion to ease transition to civilian life. Are these considerations a valid basis for adhering to early retirement provisions? Some think not.

The contention that twenty-year retirement sustains a young and vigorous force is open to debate. In 1975, 93 percent of all enlisted personnel who retired were working in noncombat jobs (those not included in the infantry, gun crew, and seamanship occupational category) and close to 31 percent of them had *never* worked in combat-related positions.[14] Thus, to the extent that the retirement system served to maintain youth and vigor, it did so in jobs for which aptitude, maturity, and experience counted more than the physical characteristics associated with youth. The President's Commission, while taking issue with an undue emphasis on youth and vigor, concluded that even if a vigorous force is desired, "the current military retirement is a clumsy means of ensuring [it]."[15]

There is virtually no evidence to support the view that early retirement provisions play a major role in *attracting* new recruits to the armed forces.

13. Memorandum, General Counsel of the Department of Defense to Walter F. Mondale, president of the Senate, July 18, 1979, transmitting legislative proposal "To amend title 10 and certain other titles, of the United States Code, to establish a new Retirement Benefits System for the Uniformed Services, and for other purposes."

14. *Report to the Congress by the Comptroller General of the United States: The 20-Year Military Retirement System Needs Reform* (General Accounting Office, 1978), pp. 9, 29. These results, while based on a limited sample, are consistent with our findings that roughly 90 percent of the enlisted personnel who retired in fiscal 1977 and 1978 were serving in noncombat assignments (based on data provided by Office of Assistant Secretary of Defense for Manpower, Reserve Affairs, and Logistics).

15. *Report of the President's Commission on Military Compensation*, p. 55.

On the contrary, an Air Force survey indicates that retirement benefits are considered relatively unimportant by members of the armed forces at least until they reach their seventh year of service.[16] Obviously retirement is an inducement in retaining more senior personnel, but its strength is difficult to measure.[17] Moreover, it seems inappropriate to offer identical incentives to retain individuals regardless of their skills. Doing so implies that everyone in the same cohort is making the same contribution to national defense and that the cost of replacement is the same for each member of that group.

Early retirement is often argued to be justified because of the special characteristics of military life—the so-called x factor. According to a former service secretary, "implicit in this concept of military service must be long-term security and a system of institutional supports for the serviceman and his family which are beyond the level of compensation commonly offered in the private, industrial sector."[18]

But the President's Commission after analyzing the retirement system concluded that it was

out of balance with most other retirement systems and an unfair burden on American taxpayers. . . . *We find no compelling evidence that the calling to a military career is sufficiently unique to justify the current system.* Likewise, we are not persuaded that the military is so special and different as to invalidate comparisons with other retirement systems. Finally, in view of the many years prior to 1945 when the military functioned without the current system . . . we reject the notion that the current system is a fundamental underpinning of the military way of life.[19]

And although recognizing the overall disadvantage that the conditions of military service impose, the Defense Manpower Commission recommended that *"there should be no explicit payment . . . made to all or most*

---

16. Ibid., p. 51.

17. Generally, individuals attach greater significance to benefits received now than to prospective future benefits; the further in the future the benefits are received, the less the significance attached to them. This time preference can be represented by the interest rate that a person is willing to pay for consumption now rather than for consumption later and is best represented by relevant alternatives in the private market. The appropriate rate of interest to use, however, is a most difficult conceptual problem on which economists differ sharply.

18. Ibid., p. 176.

19. Quoted by Lieutenant General Benjamin O. Davis, Jr., U.S. Air Force (Retired), in ibid., p. 179. Emphasis in original. Ten of the twenty-four members of the commission staff were active-duty military personnel, including the associate director for retirement studies.

Service members which is specifically designated as compensation for the X factor."[20] It noted that

in the private sector, there are many occupations or assignments entailing relatively onerous working conditions which employees must be induced to voluntarily accept. For example, laborers are employed to work on oil drilling rigs under widely varying working conditions. Most of them work on land. Others work on offshore platforms; they may live on the platform for an entire week. Others work at remote locations, such as Prudhoe Bay, for several consecutive months. Volunteers are attracted by paying differentials only to those individuals who experience the more onerous working conditions and only for the period during which these conditions are experienced. This policy is consistent with the principles recommended by the Commission with respect to military personnel.[21]

General William E. Dupuy, a retired Army officer who served as a member of the President's Commission, supported the idea of deferred compensation, calling it

a great improvement over "early retirement" systems. I say this for several reasons. First, 20-year retirement is a misnomer. Very few service members in fact retire—they go to work for somebody else. Secondly, the idea of 40-year-old people "retiring" is repugnant to the taxpayer and incompatible with the American work ethic. Deferred compensation, on the other hand, is designed to recognize and at least partially offset the arduous nature of military service.[22]

It has long been taken for granted that military retirees suffer an earnings penalty as an aftereffect of their military service. Only recently has the proposition that this justifies relatively large annuities for members of the armed forces been examined closely. A study for the President's Commission found that enlisted retirees with a high school education working full time earned from 1 percent to 24 percent less than their civilian counterparts, depending on such factors as the retiree's age (and hence on how long he had been retired), occupation, and geographic location.[23] A more extensive survey found that, when compared with the earnings of nonretired veterans of comparable age and education, "retirees' second-career earnings losses appear small, on the average [and]. . . . for many

20. *Defense Manpower*, p. 341. Emphasis in original.
21. Ibid.
22. From the text of a letter sent by General William E. Depuy, U.S. Army (Retired), to Chairman Charles J. Zwick, appearing in *Report of the President's Commission on Military Compensation*, p. 169.
23. William J. Raduchel and others, "Post-Retirement Income and Earnings of Military Personnel Who Retired from 1970 to 1974," in *Supplementary Papers of the President's Commission on Military Compensation* (GPO, 1978).

subgroups of retirees, there does not seem to be any second-career earnings loss at all."[24] Moreover, those who do sustain losses often appear to do so by choice. "Except during the five- or six-year transition period following retirement, when military retirees appear to be at a genuine disadvantage relative to their nonretired peers, any second-career loss can, on the average, be attributed to voluntary decisions made by the retiree."[25]

Low earnings after retirement do not seem to be a reasonable justification for a generous retirement annuity. Financial penalties may exist for a relatively short period of time after retirement for *many* retirees. And they may endure for a good number of years for *some* retirees. But extending early and generous benefits to *all* retirees is an extremely inefficient way of dealing with the residual problem.

Cash to Go or Cash to Stay?

Five of the recent major studies have recognized the need for annuities to be vested earlier than the twenty-year point. The 1971 Interagency Committee found that "the majority of members who separate before retirement receive nothing for the equity they have accumulated in the system."[26]

Those who advocate earlier vesting to remove the all-or-nothing feature of the current system also envisage a reduction in the number of people who would serve twenty years and hence a reduction in the number of early retirees. With a vested equity, persons with, say, ten to fifteen years of service are expected to be less inclined to "stay for twenty." And military managers would be less reticent to reduce the ranks among those who have served less than twenty years.

The earlier studies, for the most part, proposed vesting provisions similar in many respects to those included in civilian systems, both public and private. Most of the groups advocated that those members of the armed forces with between ten and nineteen years of service be entitled to a deferred, age-related annuity, as federal civilian employees are. The

---

24. Richard V. L. Cooper, *Military Retirees' Post-Service Earnings and Employment,* R-2493-MRAL (Santa Monica, Calif.: Rand Corp., 1980).

25. Ibid. The decisions referred to are those related to working hours and to geographical location.

26. *Report of the President on the Study by the Interagency Committee,* vol. 1 p. I-6. About seven of every eight recruits who enter the armed forces leave before reaching retirement eligibility.

various groups split on the question of whether an option to cash in the vested equity should be extended both to those who quit and those who leave involuntarily; for example, the 1971 Interagency Committee would extend it to both groups, the Retirement Modernization bill only to those separating involuntarily. In the latter case, however, those who quit would be entitled to severance payments.

A new twist, introduced by the President's Commission in 1978, would establish a deferred compensation trust fund for each member of the armed forces who completed five years of service. Vesting would occur when the individual completed ten years, and on completing active service the member would have the option of leaving the fund in the account for withdrawal at some later date or converting it to a monthly annuity or annual payment. Moreover, this proposal would allow members who had completed ten years of service to withdraw up to half the value of their account *while still on active duty,* which ostensibly would "provide a strong incentive for many who now leave after one enlistment to stay until the tenth year."[27] In addition, those who separated without choice would be entitled to severance pay. The Uniformed Services Retirement Benefits bill of 1979 would likewise permit early withdrawal of the amount vested; it would allow *full* withdrawals at any time after completion of ten years, again whether or not the member remained in the armed forces. These two proposals place more emphasis than their predecessors on using the military retirement system as a retention mechanism. Exactly how the option allowing early cash withdrawal might affect retention is not at all clear. The President's Commission argued that while its plan

will attract more personnel to the 10-year point, losses between 10 to 15 years of service will increase as a result of vesting for the old-age annuity and the deferred compensation trust fund. Compared to the current system, in which 20 percent of enlisted members and 13 percent of officers who completed 10 years leave active service by 15 years, losses under the Commission plan during this same period are estimated to be 63 percent for enlisted persons and 53 percent for officers.[28]

These estimates, however, are subject to a healthy measure of uncertainty. For example, under the commission's assumptions yielding a low retention rate, the experience level of the armed forces, as measured by average age, declines; at moderate rates, it remains about the same; and only under high retention assumptions is a more experienced force

---

27. *Report of the President's Commission on Military Compensation,* p. 69.
28. Ibid., pp. 83–84.

achieved. At bottom, the commission admitted that "its retirement plan will have manning effects which are sufficiently uncertain to warrant caution."[29]

Uncertainty also pervades the administration's version of the trust fund concept, but its proposal, the Defense Department contends, would "on balance, provide a force as experienced and as youthful as today's."[30]

Apart from the uncertainty of its effect on retention, the proposal can be challenged on even more fundamental grounds. It extends the option of early withdrawal to all military personnel, regardless of branch of service, occupation, or proclivity to remain in the armed forces. Thus it shares with the across-the-board pay mechanisms the shortcoming that it risks offering more than necessary to attract some and less than necessary to lure others.

Aligning Military and Federal Civilian Old-Age Benefits

For old-age security—the primary purpose that the military retirement system should serve—the plan now covering the federal civilian work force presents a possible, logical, and in many ways reasonable prototype. Since military pay has been brought roughly into line with federal civilian pay, so could the retirement system for military personnel be realigned. Federal civilian personnel may retire at the age of sixty-two with a minimum of five years of service; at sixty with twenty years; and at fifty-five with thirty years. Law enforcement workers and firefighters with twenty years of service may retire at age fifty. Early retirement with twenty-five years of service at any age is permitted when an agency is undergoing a major reduction in force. And federal civilians who are involuntarily separated without cause are entitled to an immediate annuity on attaining age fifty and completing twenty years of service or on completing twenty-five years of service, regardless of age.[31] After serving a minimum of five years, those who retire early—before becoming eligible for an immediate annuity—have an option of leaving their credit in the retirement fund and

29. Ibid., p. 128.

30. "DOD's New Proposed Military Retirement Plan," *Command Policy*, vol. 2 (July 1979), p. 9.

31. If the employee is under age 55 when retiring (either voluntarily or involuntarily without cause) the annuity rate is reduced by one sixth of 1 percent for each full month that the employee is under age 55.

drawing deferred annuity benefits on attaining the appropriate age, or of withdrawing their contribution.

Among the recent proposals to reform military retirement, the recommendations of the Defense Manpower Commission come closest to mirroring the federal civilian system. And, apart from the provisions of a trust fund, particularly as regards its withdrawal features, the President's Commission proposal is patterned closely after the federal civilian model. But Congress need not search beyond its own Congressional Budget Office (CBO) to find the makings of a viable plan. Of four options considered in a recent CBO study of the military retirement system, one comes close to being a mirror image of the federal civilian plan.[32]

Under the CBO's "annuity-at-55 option," the age eligibility rules for military retirement would be the same as those currently in effect for federal civilians (see table 5-3); but unlike federal civilians, military retirees would be eligible for an immediate annuity when reaching the appropriate age, regardless of whether they were on active duty when they reached that age. This plan would also differ from the civilian system in that military personnel still would not contribute explicitly to their retirement. And any military person who was involuntarily separated before serving thirty years would be paid a cash bonus and be eligible for a deferred annuity.

In laying out this option, the CBO stated that it

would modify the entire pattern of military careers. Fewer personnel would tend to complete 20 years of service. But many more of those who do complete 20 years' service would probably stay for careers of 30 or more years, which would lead to an older career force. Thus, this option seems most consistent with a judgment that the military can accomplish its missions with older careerists. The option also offers the potential for large cost savings, though the amount of savings would depend critically on changes in career patterns and accompanying changes in personnel management.[33]

A RETIREMENT PLAN that encouraged longer careers would be an appropriate accompaniment to a pay policy designed to attract a more mature force that is better prepared to accomplish the military mission. While early vesting of annuities might induce losses among personnel in the middle grades, everything else being equal, restructuring pay policy to

32. Congressional Budget Office, *The Military Retirement System: Options for Change,* Budget Issue Paper for Fiscal Year 1979 (GPO, 1978), pp. 27–39.

33. Ibid., p. 60.

Table 5-3. Provisions of Federal Civilian, Military, and Proposed Military Retirement Systems

Provision	Federal civilian system	Military system	Proposed military system
Retirement base	Average highest 3 years' pay	Terminal basic pay	Average highest 3 years' basic pay
Voluntary separation			
Formula for computing annuity	Retirement base times 1.5 percent per year for first 5 years of service, plus 1.25 percent per year for second 5 years, plus 2 percent per year for each year over 10 (maximum 80 percent)	Retirement base times 2.5 percent per year of service (maximum 75 percent)	Retirement base times 2.5 percent per year of service (maximum 87.5 percent)
When annuity begins	At least 30 years of service, at age 55 or over; at least 20 years, age 60 or over; at least 5 years, age 62 or over	Upon retirement with more than 20 years of service	At least 30 years of service, age 55 or over; at least 20 years, age 60 or over; at least 5 years, age 62 or over
Involuntary separation			
Formula for computing annuity	At least 25 years of service, at any age; at least 20 years, at age 50 or over (annuity reduced by 0.1667 percent for each full month employee is under age 55)	Enlisted personnel, no annuity; officers, lump-sum payment of 10 percent times years of service times retirement base (maximum of $15,000)	More than 5 years of service, same as voluntary plus lump-sum payment equal to 5 percent per year times terminal basic pay; less than 5 years, no benefits

Sources: Congressional Budget Office, *The Military Retirement System: Options for Change,* Budget Issue Paper for Fiscal Year 1979 (GPO, 1978), app. table A; Joseph Young, ed., *Federal Employees Almanac, 1979* (Merrifield, Va.: Federal Employees' News Digest, Inc., 1979), pp. 48–52.

strengthen incentives to stay in the service for those persons serving in the most demanding occupations would be a cost-effective counterbalance.[34]

The proposal to align more closely the military and the federal civilian retirement plans would be far less complicated, and thus less difficult to sell, than the other proposed retirement schemes.[35] It also would promise earlier and larger savings, which could be applied to the pay incentives necessary to retain the personnel the armed forces need most. A package deal encompassing both retirement reform and pay reform would improve the chances of garnering the support of the military rank and file. Indeed, military retirement reform would appear to be a reasonable goal.

---

34. While retention incentives of some form would be needed as a quid pro quo for the retirement reform, this does not necessarily mean that complete restructuring of military compensation would be a prerequisite. Differential bonus payments or other incentives could be used selectively to retain mid-level personnel.

35. In fact, a successful prototype is provided by the Civil Service Reform Act of 1978, 92 Stat. 1111. This legislation shared many of the shortcomings of recent military retirement proposals—complexity, uncertain financial implications, and the absence of a large or vocal constituency—and yet it was successful, in large part because of high-level interest and a strong lobby. The role of Alan K. Campbell, chairman of the U.S. Civil Service Commission, in shepherding the legislation through Congress is well recognized. Also, President Jimmy Carter took a personal interest, probably occasioned by the symbolism that the success of this particular legislation held for his administration's relations with Congress.

CHAPTER SIX

SUMMING UP

THE LOSS of seasoned specialists and trained technicians in the nation's armed forces, added to the recruitment shortfalls since the transition to an all-volunteer force in the 1970s, has taken a noticeable toll on the readiness of U.S. military forces. Widespread fear that the setbacks cannot be reversed appears to be forcing a choice between increasing the military payroll, returning to conscription, or reducing the size of the armed forces. But a better response may be to make the military compensation system more efficient.

At issue is a system of pay that is anchored to principles of institutionalism and paternalism. Instead of paying workers strictly according to their contribution, the armed forces continue to use a compensation arrangement, as old as the Republic itself, that was tailored to a force of unskilled personnel serving as foot soldiers or ablebodied seamen. Under those conditions, rank served as a reliable gauge of contribution. And even in the twentieth century, as technological developments shaped an industrialized military force calling for a great many highly trained technicians, specialists, and craftsmen, the arrangement has been taken for granted. This was understandable as long as conscription allowed the military to operate in a setting virtually unaffected by the rules of the marketplace. But since the end of the draft in 1973, the armed forces have become an employer vying for manpower in the labor market.

Their compensation system provides little in the way of efficient tools and mechanisms to improve attraction and retention of enlisted personnel. Military pay and benefits have little relevance to occupational requirements and corresponding training costs, and even less resemblance to civilian rates for workers possessing similar skills. By compensating their members, across the board and regardless of occupational area, on the basis of longevity, the armed forces inadvertently overpay some and shortchange others. The military retirement system, one of the armed services' principal retention inducements, is as indiscriminate in its effect as the pay system. The manpower imbalances—if not in numbers, certainly in quality—that the pay and retirement systems impose are a serious threat to military effectiveness and the defense budget.

Reform of the pay system is essential if the caliber of the military force is to improve and its effectiveness to be enhanced. Pay should be brought in line with the nature of the occupation, the job setting, the cost of investment in manpower training, and, where appropriate, with alternative employment opportunities and earnings prevailing in the civilian economy. Pay distinctions based on occupation should be incorporated in the structure of regular military compensation, and the traditional link between rank, pay grade, and occupation should be severed. This would require no change in either the existing pay tables or the distribution of rank titles among enlisted members. It would depend on realignment of the grade structure of jobs. The separation of rank and grade would preserve rank as an important institutional feature while providing for differential opportunities for grade advancement. Pay grades could then be allocated in a manner consistent with the nature and requirements of military jobs, with the number of top grades proportionately greater in those occupations where longer careers are more appropriate. Should more enlisted technicians and craftsmen find greater appeal in longer careers, manpower utilization in the armed forces would be certain to improve.

In conjunction with the restructuring of the pay system for the military work force, the urgently needed reform in the retirement system appears promising. The system, which should be geared principally to provide old-age security, can be most efficiently realigned by providing for military personnel to retire in much the same way as their civilian counterparts do. Modernizing military retirement in this fashion promises to be relatively uncomplicated, and if linked with pay reform, it stands a good chance of gaining the support of legislators and of the defense establishment.

CAUGHT BETWEEN the demands of an increasingly technological military establishment on the one hand, and the growing difficulties in the recruitment and retention of qualified personnel on the other, decisionmakers sooner or later must come to grips with the problems of an out-of-date pay policy. The manning problems of the late 1970s and early 1980s, if they persist, will hasten the showdown. Recasting military compensation policies in such a way as to render the pay structure more competitive with that prevailing in the civilian economy could go a long way toward shaping a force more closely matched to the demands of the modern military establishment.

Statistical Tables

Table A-1. Distribution of Trained Military Enlisted Personnel, by Occupational Category, 1945, 1957, and 1977

Percent

Occupational category[a]	1945	1957	1977
White collar	28	40	46
Technical workers[b]	13	21	28
Clerical workers[e]	15	19	18
Blue collar	72[d]	60	55
Craftsmen[e]	29	32	27
Service and supply workers	17	13	12
Infantry, gun crews, and seamanship specialists	24	15	16

Sources: Harold Wool, *The Military Specialist: Skilled Manpower for the Armed Forces* (Johns Hopkins Press, 1968), table III-3, p. 42; data provided by U.S. Department of Defense, Office of Assistant Secretary of Defense for Manpower, Reserve Affairs, and Logistics. Percentages are rounded.

a. Based on Department of Defense occupational classification system.

b. In 1945 and 1957 includes "electronics" and "other technical" categories; in 1977 includes "electronic equipment repairmen," "communications and intelligence specialists," "medical and dental specialists," and "other technical and allied specialists" categories.

c. In 1945 and 1957 includes administrative and clerical personnel; in 1977 is the "functional support and administration" category.

d. Includes 2 percent classified as miscellaneous.

e. In 1945 and 1957 includes "mechanics and repairmen" and "craftsmen" categories; in 1977 includes "electrical/mechanical equipment repairmen" and "craftsmen" categories.

Table A-2. Distribution of Civilian Sector Workers and Military Personnel, by Occupational Category, 1977

Percent

Occupational category	Civilian sector workers		Military personnel	
	Total	Male	Total[a]	Enlisted
Common to both sectors				
Technicians	15[b]	15[b]	30[b]	28[c]
Managers and administrators	10	14	3	[d]
Clerical workers	18	6	15	18[e]
Craftsmen	13	21	23	27[f]
Service workers	14	9	10	12[g]
Mainly confined to one sector				
Tactical operations officers and infantry, gun crews, and seamanship specialists	...	...	19	16
Farm workers	3	4	...	...
Sales workers	6	6	...	...
Other (operatives and nonfarm workers)	20	25	...	...

Sources: Data provided by Office of Assistant Secretary of Defense for Manpower, Reserve Affairs, and Logistics; U.S. Department of Labor, Bureau of Labor Statistics, *Employment and Earnings*, vol. 25 (May 1978), table A-22, p. 35. Percentages are rounded.

a. Includes officers. General officers and executives; administrators; and supply, procurement, and allied officers are classified as managers and administrators. Intelligence; engineering and maintenance; and scientific, professional, and medical officers are classified as professional workers.

b. Includes professional workers.

c. Includes electronic equipment repairmen, communications and intelligence specialists, medical and dental specialists; and other technical and allied specialists.

d. A few enlisted positions may involve some administrative duties, apart from the supervisory responsibilities of staff at the E-8 and E-9 grade levels. However, because it is difficult to distinguish between supervisors and administrators among enlisted personnel, and because officers include a relatively well-defined class of managers and administrators in the military, managerial positions are assumed here—perhaps at the risk of oversimplification—to be filled by officers.

e. "Functional support and administration" category.

f. Includes "electrical/mechanical equipment repairmen"'and "craftsmen" categories.

g. "Service and supply handlers" category.

Table A-3. Age Distribution of Male Military Personnel on Active Duty, Selected Years, 1920–76[a]

Percent

	Male military personnel on active duty						
Age	*1920*	*1930*	*1940*[b]	*1950*	*1960*	*1970*	*1976*
Under 20	23.4	13.3	19.0	19.1	17.1	13.6	16.8
20–24	37.3	36.8	40.9	36.2	36.7	49.7	37.0
Over 24	39.3	49.9	40.1	44.7	46.3	36.7	46.2
Median	23.0	24.0	24.0	24.0	24.0	23.0	24.0

Sources: U.S. Bureau of the Census, *Fourteenth Census of the United States Taken in the Year 1920*, vol. 4: *Population 1920, Occupations* (Government Printing Office, 1923), table 6, pp. 392–93; *Fifteenth Census of the United States: 1930, Population*, vol. 5: *General Report on Occupations* (GPO, 1933), table 6, pp. 132–33; *Sixteenth Census of the United States: 1940, Population*, vol. 3: *The Labor Force: Occupation, Industry, Employment, and Income* (GPO, 1943), pt. 1: *United States Summary*, table 65, p. 99. U.S. Department of Defense, Office of Assistant Secretary, Comptroller, *Selected Manpower Statistics, 1973* (DOD, 1973), p. 39, and *1977* (DOD, 1977), table 311B, pp. 42–43.

a. Data, except for 1940, include both officers and enlisted personnel; data in table 1-1, above, pertain to enlisted personnel only.

b. Excludes commissioned officers, professional and clerical workers, and craftsmen.

Table A-4. Age Distribution of Military Enlisted Personnel and Civilian Sector Male Workers, by Occupational Category, 1977

Percent

	Age			
Occupational category	*17–24*[a]	*25–34*	*35–44*	*Over 44*
Military enlisted personnel[b]				
Technical workers	53	33	13	1
Clerical workers	43	36	18	2
Craftsmen	59	29	11	1
Other	64	26	10	1
Civilian sector male workers				
Technical workers[c]	10	35	23	32
Clerical workers	25	25	16	34
Craftsmen	17	27	21	35
Other[d]	40	20	13	28

Sources: Data provided by Office of Assistant Secretary of Defense for Manpower, Reserve Affairs, and Logistics, and by Bureau of Labor Statistics. Percentages are rounded.

a. Civilian percentages include 16-year-olds.

b. Categories defined in table A-1, plus "other," which includes "service and supply handlers" and "infantry, gun crews, and seamanship specialists" categories.

c. Includes professional occupations.

d. Nonfarm laborers and service workers.

Table A-5. Basic Monthly Rates of Pay of Military Enlisted Personnel, by Grade, October 1, 1980

Dollars per month

Pay grade	Under 2	2	3	4	6	8	10	12	14	16	18	20	22	26
									Years of service					
E-9	...	...	...	...	...	...	1,413.60	1,445.70	1,478.40	1,512.60	1,546.20	1,576.20	1,659.30	1,820.40
E-8	...	...	...	...	...	1,185.90	1,219.20	1,251.60	1,284.30	1,317.90	1,348.50	1,381.50	1,462.80	1,626.00
E-7	828.00	893.70	927.00	959.10	992.10	1,023.30	1,056.30	1,089.00	1,138.20	1,170.60	1,203.60	1,219.20	1,301.10	1,462.80
E-6	715.20	779.70	812.40	846.60	878.10	910.20	943.50	992.10	1,023.30	1,056.30	1,072.20	1,072.20	1,072.20	1,072.20
E-5	627.90	683.40	716.40	747.60	796.50	828.90	862.20	893.70	910.20	910.20	910.20	910.20	910.20	910.20
E-4	603.60	637.50	674.70	727.20	756.00	756.00	756.00	756.00	756.00	756.00	756.00	756.00	756.00	756.00
E-3	580.50	612.30	636.90	662.10	662.10	662.10	662.10	662.10	662.10	662.10	662.10	662.10	662.10	662.10
E-2	558.60	558.60	558.60	558.60	558.60	558.60	558.60	558.60	558.60	558.60	558.60	558.60	558.60	558.60
E-1	501.30	501.30	501.30	501.30	501.30	501.30	501.30	501.30	501.30	501.30	501.30	501.30	501.30	501.30

Source: *Army Times*, September 22, 1980.